PORCUPINE MOUNTAINS WILDERNESS STATE PARK

A Backcountry Guide For Hikers, Campers, Backpackers And Skiers

SECOND EDITION

Other Books By Jim DuFresne:

Isle Royale: Foot Trails & Water Routes

Michigan State Parks

Michigan's Best Outdoor Adventures With Children

50 Hikes In Lower Michigan

Wild Michigan

Lower Michigan's Best 75 Campgrounds

Tramping In New Zealand

Backpacking In Alaska

Alaska: A Travel Survival Kit

Glacier Bay National Park: A Backcountry Guide To The Glaciers And Beyond

PORCUPINE MOUNTAINS WILDERNESS STATE PARK

A Backcountry Guide For Hikers, Campers, Backpackers And Skiers

By Jim DuFresne

PEGG LEGG
PUBLICATIONS

Porcupine Mountains Wilderness State Park

Second Edition
Published by Thunder Bay Press
Production and maps by Pegg Legg Publications
Editing by Jean Daily

©1999 by Jim DuFresne
First Edition 1993
Second Revised Edition 1999

All rights reserved under International and Pan American
Copyright Conventions. No part of this book may be reproduced
in any manner whatsoever without written permission from the
author, except in the case of brief quotations embodied in
reviews and articles.

Printed in the United States of America

03   02   01   5   4   3   2

ISBN 1-882376-64-1

Thunder Bay Press
P.O. Box 580
Holt, Michigan 48842 USA

To Jessica,
A very special book about a very special place
for a very special person.
j.d.

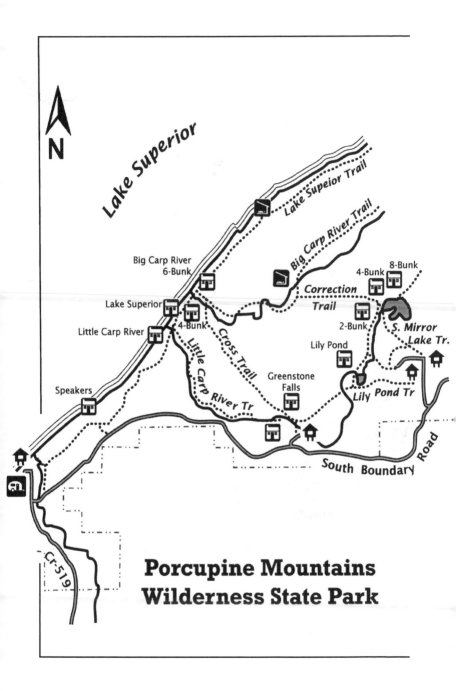

N

Lake Superior

Lake Superior Trail

Big Carp River Trail

Big Carp River
6-Bunk

4-Bunk   8-Bunk

Correction
Trail

Lake Superior

2-Bunk   S. Mirror
Lake Tr.

Little Carp River   4-Bunk

Lily Pond

Cross Trail

Speakers

Little Carp River Tr

Greenstone
Falls

Lily Pond Tr

Road

South Boundary

Cr-519

**Porcupine Mountains
Wilderness State Park**

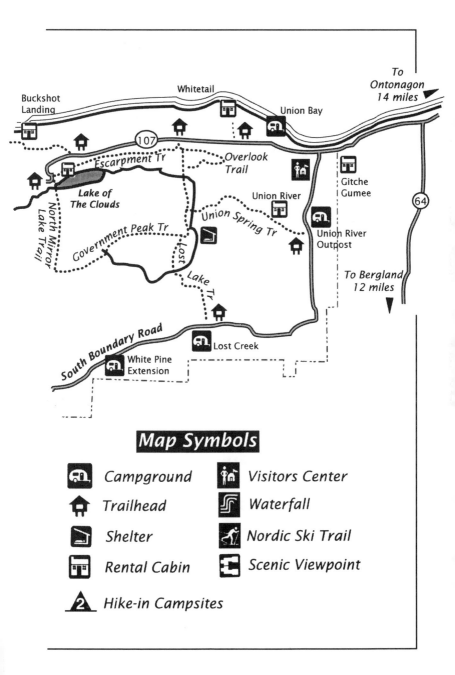

Buckshot Landing

Whitetail

Union Bay

To Ontonagon 14 miles

107

Escarpment Tr

Overlook Trail

Lake of The Clouds

North Mirror Lake Trail

Government Peak Tr

Union River

Gitche Gumee

Union Spring Tr

Lost Lake Tr

64

Union River Outpost

To Bergland 12 miles

South Boundary Road

Lost Creek

White Pine Extension

Map Symbols

Campground

Trailhead

Shelter

Rental Cabin

Hike-in Campsites

Visitors Center

Waterfall

Nordic Ski Trail

Scenic Viewpoint

CONTENTS

Acknowledgments

In Michigan, maybe in all of the Midwest, there is no place like the Porkies. This rugged land of ridges, bluffs and high points is truly one of the great tracts of wilderness in our portion of the country. Its history is colorful, its trail are challenging, its character wild even to those who are simply passing through.

I deeply appreciate Ron Welton's invitation to undertake this project, the time he spent proofing the manuscript and the encouragement he provided to finish the book once we began. If nothing else comes from this endeavor, the opportunity to hike all the trails and work with one of the finest park managers in the state is reward enough for me.

I am forever indebted to my editor, Jean Daily, who took on these pages with two red pens and the largest dictionary she could find. She's proof you don't need to own a pair of hiking boots to know a dangling participial in the woods when you see one.

No expedition can be possible without the enduring equipment of my sponsors; Kelty and its wonderful Windfoil tent, the famed MSR stove from Mountain Safety Research, Dana packs, the Equalizer sleeping pad from Basic Designs and the world's best outdoor clothing from Patagonia.

Some of this material first appeared as articles in the Venture Outdoors section of Booth Newspapers and for that I thank my editor at Booth News Service in Lansing,

And finally to my hiking partners, who endured the rain, wicked downhill runs on cross country skis and three mice in Buckshot Landing Cabin...the book is mine but the Porkies are yours.

j.d.

Forward

Porcupine Mountains Wilderness State Park is one of Michigan's truly special places. These midwestern "mountains" on the south shore of Lake Superior are home to both the country's largest remaining stand of old growth Northern hardwoods and middle America's wildest whitewater, the Presque Isle.

Though wilderness preservation remains a primary mission, facilities have been developed to serve the wide diversity of park visitors to our largest state park. Those not wishing to hike miles into the park interior can enjoy wilderness panoramas, waterfalls, and scenic vistas just short walks from parking areas. Campers enjoy sites right on Lake Superior's shores, with a variety of amenities. Scenic beauty envelops downhill and cross-country skiers from groomed trails. The Visitor Center presents a variety of interpretive programs.

Jim DuFresne provides a wealth of information to help you plan and enjoy your trip. You will discover his book is valuable both in preparation four your trip and reference during your visits. The more you understand the Porkies, the more you will appreciate this rugged yet accessible area.

The park staff is also committed to enhancing your trip. Please seek us out should you encounter any problems. Visitors' questions, comments and concerns are always important to us. Welcome to a Michigan wilderness; welcome to Porcupine Mountains Wilderness State Park.

Ron Welton
Park Manager

A backpacker views Lake of the Clouds from the Escarpment Trail.

1 A Place Called The Porkies

Something moved.

In the shadowy light of a full moon, my task of filling the water bottles was interrupted when in the corner of my eye I saw movement on the other side of Little Carp River.

Or I thought I did.

I studied the black trunks of the hardwoods and pines, the silhouettes of bushes and stumps, but on this October evening all was quiet and still in the heart of the Porcupine Mountains. I was on the verge of returning to my chore when a shadow moved again; three steps this way, one step that way. It stopped; I stood up. It turned towards me; I peered into the darkness at it. And suddenly we were both conscious of each other.

Man meets bear in a place called the Porkies.

We both might have bolted into the woods, but 20 yards of rushing water gave us a sense of security so we took the opportunity to study each other a little bit longer. The few black bears I had encountered in Michigan looked little more than a large dog. This one had some bulk to it...a 250-pound bear? Maybe a 300-pounder? And when it turned sideways the shadow the moonlight cast of my backwoods companion was even more impressive.

"Whoa!" I said softly under my breath.

It inched closer to the riverbank, nuzzled this with its nose, pawed that with its claws, and then stopped again to look at me. Only 30 yards separated us and now the bear appeared to be squinting at me.

"Gotta go," I said in a booming voice so there was no question in its mind as to what I was. I retreated up the bank in three steps or less, and after reaching the top I turned to the river again.

The bear was gone. It vanished into the shadows from which it emerged without leaving a trace of its movement.

I sat down on a stump and wondered what else was out there when the spirit of this wilderness descended upon me, like it always does at such moments. It's not picturesque Lake of the Clouds or the views from Summit Peak, as nice as they are, that make some of us return year after year to Porcupine Mountains Wilderness State Park. It's the feeling of being out there in a land where man is at best a visitor passing through. It's the idea that this rugged corner of the Upper Peninsula has been explored and mapped and even laced with foot trails and backcountry cabins, but never tamed. Like a fortress against development and that oxymoron we call "progress", the Porkies have always been this place where you retreated to rediscover yourself and the natural world around you.

It's a timeless quality first experienced by the Indians and then acknowledged by those early miners. Today it's a priceless quality that attracts thousands of visitors who merely want to wander down a path or pause in wonder along the rocky shoreline of Lake Superior. The billboards, the golden arches, the motorized pace of our society is somewhere else.

Out here it's towering pines 300 years old and spectacular waterfalls. It's sweeping views from rocky knobs reached by the slow and thoughtful pace of foot travel that keeps everything in proper perspective.

If only for a few days, leave your vehicle, slow down and look around. There's a bear on the other side of the river.

A Place Called The Porkies

The Porcupine Mountains, like Isle Royale, the Keweenaw Peninsula and much of the Lake Superior basin was born during the Precambrian era, some 1.2 billion years ago when lava seeped up through the cracks of the earth and formed basalt, the bedrock of the area. After each lava flow, wind and rain carried sand, gravel and other sediments, producing layers of soft rock between the hard slabs of basalt.

A hiker crosses Big Carp River on the way to Lake Superior.

Eventually the center began to subside and this warp, called the Lake Superior Syncline, created the basin of the Great Lake while the raised and titled layers of rock became its borders. Over thousands of years the bands of basalt have withstood forces of nature to remain as ridges while the softer layers of rock eroded away to form the valleys and inland lakes between them.

Nowhere is this more evident then the Escarpment along Lake Superior, known by geologists at the Outer or Great Conglomerate. The domal warp resulted in a ridge that rises 900 feet above Lake Superior and then gives way to a 400-foot escarpment leading to the valley that contains Lake of the Clouds and Carp Creek. This pattern is repeated in a more subdued form to give the park its "mountainous" topography.

Technically the Porkies are not mountains. A geologist defines such topography as a spot 2,000 feet or higher. The highest point in the state park is Summit Peak which at 1,958 feet is one of the highest "mountains" between the Black Hills of South Dakota and New York's Adirondacks but still 42 feet short of fulfilling a geologist's definition. True mountain or not, backpackers today still take notice of the sharp climbs to the top of the ridges and so did the Native Americans. The eroded edges of the park's escarpment and the gentle northern slope to Lake Superior were described by the first Indians as "crouched porcupines," hence the name Porcupine Mountains.

Indians began wandering into the area as early as 1750 B.C. They struggled over the ridges and escarpments during the summer in an effort to mine copper. Using fire and water, they fractured boulders, pounded out the metal and shaped it into tools, ornaments and projectile points. Some archaeologists have estimated that the ancient miners extracted more than 500 million pounds of copper from an area that included the Porkies, Isle Royale and the Keweenaw Peninsula and then traded it throughout Eastern North America.

But it was not copper that brought the first Europeans into the area, rather furs. The great North American fur trade that spread across the Great Lakes in the late 1700's was responsible for the first white settlements in the Porkies in the form of trading posts at the outlets of the Iron and Presque Isle Rivers. The bands of Ojibway Indians soon forgot their clay pots and copper tools for the guns, iron kettles, and axes they could obtain with beaver pelts and other furs.

By 1837 the fur trade was winding down when Michigan became a state. That year its young Governor, Stevens T. Mason, appointed Douglas Houghton as State Geologist and appropriated funds for a geological survey to map's the Upper Peninsula's unknown wealth of natural resources.

Houghton and his team accomplished a great deal during their journey. They collected plant and mineral specimens, mapped swamps, rivers and lakes, reported on timber and the quality of soil.

Whitetail Deer pause to look behind them out of curiosity.

However it was his geological survey that drew the most attention. It was published in 1841 and told of the copper deposits in the Western U.P. One man's report, yet it was all that was needed to create the first great mining rush in American history as men swarmed into copper country in search of fortunes they were sure were hidden in the rocks.

The first mining effort in the Porkies was the Union Mine that was started in 1845 as the Isle Royale and Lake Superior Mine near the Union River. William W. Spalding was in charge of the operation, and the remains of the first shaft can still be seen today along the Union Mine Trail near interpretive post number 1. Spalding eventually found a vein of cooper but little profit was ever realized by the early investors.

In 1864 the company was sold to a Detroit businessman. Four more shafts were sunk, one up to 400 feet deep, and a steam powered stamping mill used for crushing ore was brought in. Eventually the entire operation was given up due to exorbitant production and shipping costs versus the low grade of ore.

This was the story for the 45 mines started in the Porcupine

Mountains. The copper veins rarely could turn a profit for the investors, who on the average spent five times more extracting the metal than it was worth on the open market. While solid cooper masses of several hundred tons were found in mines east of Ontonagon, including a pure 3,708-pound nugget known as the Ontonagon Boulder that today rests in the Smithsonian Institute, the Porkies copper existed in small particles and flakes within the rock. Without the rich veins of copper, the only time mines, like the Union, LaFayette, Halliwell and Cuyahoga, turned a profit was when the Civil War demand for the metal drove the prices high enough to overcome the production costs.

The last mine in the area was the Nonesuch, which opened in 1867. Located south of the Union Mine, the Nonesuch was operated off and on until 1910. At its peak the operation boasted a rail tram to its Union Bay docks, 12 log homes, an agent's residence, general store, post office, a stagecoach, even a uniformed baseball team. It also swallowed several large fortunes while producing only 180 tons of refined copper during its 43-year existence. Today remains of of the mine can still be viewed by continuing on a dirt road where South Boundary Road curves west, 4.3 miles south of M-107.

There were some attempts to mine silver, which proved no more profitable than copper and then in the early 1900s, as the mining era was ending, the logging began. From Lone Rock east to Cuyahoga Gap, lumberjacks concentrated on the shoreline pines but passed up the rugged interior of the Porkies for more accessible tracts elsewhere.

The only other major logging in the present park occurred following a devastating natural disaster. On the morning of June 30, 1953, tornado-force winds raged across Lake Superior and finally touched land near the mouth of the Big Carp River. The gale proceeded to cut a two-mile-wide path through the forest in which trunks two-feet in diameter were twisted and snapped like match sticks. Faced with 1,200 acres of fallen trees that represented more than 10 million board feet, the park staff allowed loggers to enter

The Porkies makes for excellent black bear habitat.

the park and salvage the wood.

The rest of the Porkies' interior remained unmolested by miners, loggers and other entrepreneurs. By the 1930s the Porcupine Mountains were a rare remnant of the virgin forest which once had stretched from the Mississippi River to the Atlantic Ocean and was soon being referred to as a "forest museum." Eventually the federal government designated the Porkies as a potential site for the next national park, but the plans were abandoned by the financially strapped Congress at the start of World War II. When the war demand for lumber renewed the loggers, interest for the interior timber, concerned citizens and the state did what the federal government could not.

Global conflict or not, this distant corner of Michigan, the largest stand of virgin maple and hemlock between the Rockies and the Adirondacks, was too precious to be stripped just for its trees. A push for the Porkies preservation resulted in it becoming a state park in 1945, and in 1946, its first year as an operational unit, Porcupine Mountains State Park drew 70,000 visitors.

State park status was not enough, however, to keep the mining and logging interests at bay. Over the years not only were developers eyeing the resources of the Porkies, but politicians proposed such schemes that ranged from building a road along Lake Superior to a push for a dog racing track in the park. The management and protection of the Porkies finally peaked in heated controversy that ended when the state passed the Wilderness and Natural Areas Act in 1972, and the park officially became known as Porcupine Mountains Wilderness State Park.

"It was almost a national park and it really is a national park quality resource," said one park manager. "Few state parks have the resource base that the Porkies have."

Or the dimensions. Although the majority of the 500,000 annual visitors never venture beyond the Lake of the Clouds overlook, a spectacular vista of a lake surrounded by ridges and escarpments, this park is much more than one over-photographed viewing point.

Michigan's largest state park is 26 miles long, 10 miles at its widest point and covers more than 60,000 acres. Along with peaks that top 1,900 feet, the Porkies contain 25 miles of Lake Superior shoreline, four lakes, entire rivers, trout streams that are choked with spawning salmon in the fall, and 14 waterfalls that are named, dozens more that are not.

There are also more than 90 miles of foot paths that wind through the heart of this wilderness. The longest is the Lake Superior Trail that stretches for 16 miles along the lakeshore. Others say the most scenic trek in the Upper Peninsula is the four-mile hike along the Escarpment Trail which gives way to vistas of sheer cliffs and panoramas of Lake of the Clouds.

Whether it's a half-mile walk to the Greenstone Falls or a four-day trek to the most remote corner of the park, these foot paths are the avenues to the natural treasures the Porkies have protected throughout history.

FLORA AND FAUNA

Despite the best efforts of miners and loggers, the rugged interior of the Porcupine Mountains kept most of man's activity confined to its edges and outer regions. The result is that today the Porkies support the most extensive virgin hardwood forest be-

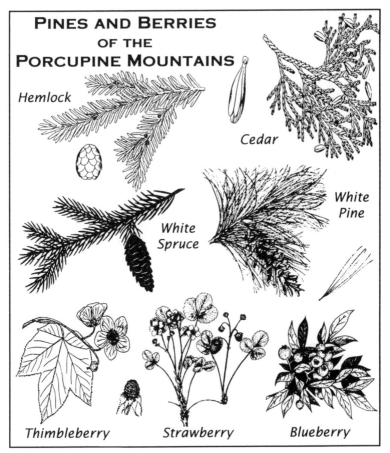

PINES AND BERRIES
OF THE
PORCUPINE MOUNTAINS

Hemlock

Cedar

White
Pine

White
Spruce

Thimbleberry   Strawberry   Blueberry

tween the Adirondacks and the Rocky Mountains.

More than one half of the state park remains virgin timber with the forest being dominated by hemlock and northern hardwoods such as sugar maple, basswood, and yellow birch. Miners eagerly sought out the yellow birch and maple for its dense wood which was used in the supporting timbers of their mines and, more importantly, the production of charcoal to fuel the steam engines in the stamp mills.

On north facing slopes hemlock becomes the dominate species and often is found in almost pure stands while swamps and low lying areas are forested by tamarack and white cedar. Miners also had an eye for the cedar as its resistance to rot when in contact with the soil made it their first choice for support beams in the shafts.

In the flood plains of the Carp Rivers and other streams you encounter white spruce and black ash while much of the area between M-107 and Lake Superior is made up of aspen and paper birch. This is the result of the heavy shoreline logging that took place in the early 1900s and the slash fires that followed, reducing the land to bare rock.

A variety of wild berries thrives in the park including bearberry and blueberry, best encountered along the crests and cliffs of the front ranges. On the forest floor there is often an abundance of thimbleberries, a tart edible fruit which is a favorite with local jam makers. The waist-high bush has a large maple-like leaf, a white blossom and berries that ripen from July to mid-August.

Wildlife in the park range from deer, fishers, river otters beavers, porcupines and red squirrels to a variety of birds including goshawks, peregrine falcons, barred owl and bald eagles. In the fall it is possible to stand on the bridge near the mouth of the Big Carp River and watch Chinook salmon gather in the pools for a spawning run upstream.

The park also supports coyotes, bobcats, pine martens and even an occasional wolf although the animal that commands the most attention here is the black bear. The rugged and wooded terrain of the Porkies is good habitat for bruins, and biologists estimate that the area supports a bear for every 4 to 5 square miles for roughly a total population that fluxiates between 15 and 25.

A two to three-year-old bear averages 150 pounds and looks like a large, rounded dog when on all fours but large males have been known to weigh in at 300 to 500 pounds. Bears are carnivorous, feeding on roots, berries, whatever they find in the woods and occasionally a deer fawn. They may appear to be slow, but bears can easily out run a person while a 200-pound bruin can crawl through an opening that would be a squeeze for even a child.

Bears begin denning in early October and are hibernating for

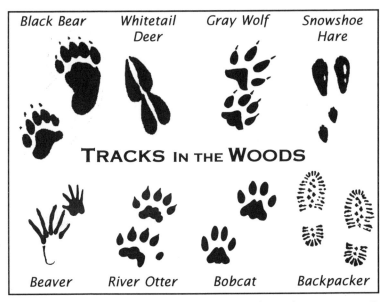

Black Bear   Whitetail Deer   Gray Wolf   Snowshoe Hare

TRACKS IN THE WOODS

Beaver   River Otter   Bobcat   Backpacker

the winter by mid-November, not emerging from their caves until March or April. Sows breed every other year with an average litter ranging from one to two cubs although biologists have recorded litters as large as five. Cubs weigh around a half pound at birth and stay with the mother through the following winter.

It's important to practice good bear precautions when staying in the park, especially if you are traveling or camping in the backcountry (see page 36). It's equally important to realize that a bear has never seriously injured a visitor in the Porkies and that a small percentage of backpackers even see them during the summer. What you will often spot are their tracks. A bear print looks more like a human foot than a dog track. But it has a more rounded pad and claws that can usually be clearly seen off the toes. A track four inches or wider is a sign of a good size bear.

While a few bruins will raid the suspended food sacks of backpackers every summer, biologists will quickly point out that most have a healthy respect for people and simply turn and run when encountered. They seen to understand there is little to gain by exposing themselves.

A backpacker pauses on a foggy morning in the Porkies.

2 Enjoying The Porkies

There is a group of us who get together to do nothing but hike and eat. We're backpacking gourmets; we may sleep on the ground but we eat like kings. We sharpen our appetite with long treks into the woods and then enjoy scrumptious meals with a view from our plate that few restaurants in Michigan can match.

One summer, with packs bulging with shallots, sour cream, and wine in a box (minus the box), we entered Porcupine Mountains Wilderness State Park for four days of gastronomic adventures.

The rules of the outing were simple. Each of us was in charge of an entire meal, from pre-trip planning and preparation to serving it and washing the pots. All ingredients had to be obtained from the average supermarket. That's especially important, for if I ate four or five days of freeze-dried "meal-in-a-pouch" dinners I'd have enough gas to drive home.

I had dinner on the third day and the culinary competition was tough. We had already eaten our way through Chicken Cacciatore, Eggs Benedict, freshly baked croissants (somebody packed in an Outback Oven for baking) and No-Bake Drop Cookies for dessert one night (clever, clever, we all remarked).

With a determination to finally capture the coveted trophy (a leftover bag of gorp), I went to work in the middle of the wilderness when we stopped for a night at the mouth of the Big Carp River. My appetizers were a selection of smoked trout and sharp cheddar cheeses served with an English hardsauce. The next course was cream of asparagus soup (dried soup mix from International Bazaar), followed by a marinated cabbage salad that was marinating as we hiked in, and the main entree of Fettuccine with Sausage Ragout Sauce.

The mouth of the Big Carp River on Lake Superior.

"How did you pack in the sweet Italian sausage?" asked one of my critics.

"It's dried sausage that I reconstituted."

"Why isn't the fettuccine all broken from three days at the bottom of your pack?" asked another.

"It's fresh pasta."

But the coup de grace came at the end. For dessert I walked down to Lake Superior and from the frigid waters pulled out a tightly sealed pot that contained individual cheese cakes (the key was the miniature Ready Crusts by Keebler). I topped off the well-chilled dessert with a fruit sauce made from dried cherries and served them with what I call "Campfire Capuccino", a hot drink that contains, among other ingredients, a Hershey chocolate bar, instant coffee, Grand Marnier and a layer of melted marshmallow at the top instead of steamed milk.

They gave me a standing ovation and the bag of half eaten gorp.

Then on the shores of Lake Superior, facing one of the most beautiful panoramas in Michigan, we indulged in dessert and after dinner drinks until the setting sun had turned the Great Lake blazing orange. And some people think wilderness treks and good cuisine are incompatible!

🚶 Visiting The Park

Porcupine Mountains Wilderness State Park draws more than 450,000 visitors annually, and from May through October when the vast majority arrive, they can easily be divided into three categories. The most common is a *day visitor*, who arrives to take in the panorama from the Lake of the Clouds Escarpment, view the exhibits at the visitor's center and possibly have a picnic along the shores of Lake Superior. Then they're off to other attractions in the U.P., often spending less than two hours in the park.

Then there are the *campers*, an estimated 100,000, who stay for a night or more in one of the five campgrounds on the edge of the park. Their journeys into the interior of the Porkies are strictly dayhikes where they can travel without the burden of having to carry heavy loads in a backpack and by nightfall are back in the comfort of a trailer or a spacious tent at their site.

Jim DuFresne's Better Trail Mix

3 Large Bags of M&Ms
1 Ziplock plastic bag

Open bags of M&Ms and pour into the plastic bag. Mix well. Hey, why not? In the world of backpackers I am known as an M&M picker. I pick out the candy first and eat the nuts and raisins only when there is nothing left. I might as well make trail mix that's nothing but M&Ms. If this puts you too much on a guilt trip then throw in a handful of those whole wheat crunches so you can call it "healthy" while still consuming entire bags of it in the backcountry.

A pair of bald eagles rest on a branch near the top of a shoreline tree
Eagles are commonly seen along the Lake Superior shoreline near the
river mouths in the park.

And finally there are the *backcountry users*, visitors who leave their cars at the trailheads. They take to the paths in order to spend every minute of their stay deep in the mountains, either by booking a trailside cabin in advance or carrying in a tent.

To get the most out of any trip to this park, it's best to know what is available and plan accordingly, especially if reservations are required. Cabins and campgrounds are covered in Chapter 3, trails in chapters 6 through 9 and the winter facilities and ski trails in chapter 10. But here are the day-use areas and other facilities:

Headquarters: The park recently relocated its headquarters across from the Visitor Center off South Boundary Road. The office is open year round, Monday through Friday from 8 a.m. to 5 p.m. and can provide maps, handle cabin and campground reservations and provide information about all the park's facilities and activities. Contact the park at ☎ (906) 885-5275 or write:

Park Manager
Porcupine Mountains Wilderness State Park
412 South Boundary Road
Ontonagon, MI 49953.

Visitor Center: The first stop for any person just arriving at the park, day visitor or backcountry user, should be the park's impressive Visitor Center, located a half mile south of M-107 on South Boundary Road. Inside there are exhibits explaining everything about the park from its creation and history of the miners to its flora and wildlife, including a display devoted to black bears. There is also a theater where a slide presentation about the park is shown throughout the day. Perhaps the most interesting item, at least to anybody who plans to hike the trails, is the three-dimensional relief map that gives one a good idea just how rugged the Porkies really are. During the summer the center is the best source for maps and trail information as well the place to go for a backcountry permit. It is open from Memorial Day to Oct. 15 from 10 a.m. until 6 p.m.

Picnic Areas: There is a picnic area on each side of the park adjacent to the two major campgrounds. On the east side, near the

Union Bay Campground, picnic tables are situated along the Lake Superior shoreline along M-107. Across the road a short trail leads to the Visitor Center. On the west side the picnic area is passed just before entering the Presque Isle Campground and includes a shelter as well as tables, vault toilets and pedestal grills. A meal here is enhanced even more with a short stroll down the boardwalk to the picturesque mouth of the Presque Isle River.

Lake of the Clouds Overlook: At the end of M-107, it's a short walk to perhaps Michigan's most famous panorama. The overlook is set on the side of the Escarpment, a vertical cliff basically, and from the high point of 1,375 feet it is possible to see the Porkies' rugged interior and the picturesque Lake of the Clouds set among the forested ridges. Displays near the parking area explain the geology of the Escarpment while three trails; Big Carp River, Escarpment and North Mirror Lake depart from here. There are picnic tables and toilets located here but no source of water.

Summit Peak Tower: The other spectacular viewing point in the park is the tower on Summit Peak, the highest point in the Porkies at 1,958 feet. A trip to the observation deck begins with a drive up the winding Summit Peak Road through virgin timber. Once on top you follow a path a half mile to the 40-foot high tower. The view spans the interior of the Porkies while on a clear day it's possible to see Copper Peak along the Black River and even Apostle Islands off Wisconsin. Facilities include tables and a toilet building but no source of water.

Permits And Fees

Whether you plan to be in the park for an hour or a week, you need to have either a daily vehicle permit or an annual state park pass. These can be purchased at various contact stations in the park, the Visitor Center or the park headquarters. A state park pass allows you unlimited entry to any unit in the Michigan State Park system for the year.

All overnight hikers must also register before embarking on their trek and each party must obtain a rustic camping permit if

Section 17 Cabin and a snowshoer in April.

they are not staying in a cabin. There is a per night fee for the permits which can be obtained at the Visitor Center, the park headquarters or the contact stations at Presque Isle or Union Bay campgrounds. If a ranger is not on duty then register at the self registration station outside the park headquarters.

🚶 Dayhiking

No permit is needed to spend a day hiking in the backcountry but you must still purchase a vehicle entry permit or an annual state park pass. Trailheads are marked on the park map and posted along M-107, South Boundary Road and at the Presque Isle day-use area. Small parking lots are near most of the trailheads although at times in mid-summer they could easily be filled with vehicles.

Even if you are only dayhiking, don't under estimate the park's ruggedness. Most day hikers need 40 minutes to an hour to cover a mile of trail, depending on their physical condition. The trails are well marked and for the most part easy to follow, but still pack along a map, drinking water, compass and a small flashlight in case you lag behind after the sun sets. Most important, bring a parka or jacket for protection against a sudden turn in the weather. The last thing you want is to get caught in the middle of the Porkies in shorts and a t-shirt when a storm blows in unexpectedly.

BACKCOUNTRY CAMPING

Unless you have reserved wilderness cabins in advance, once in the backcountry you will be either pitching a tent or staying in one of three Adirondack-style trail shelters. The three-sided shelters are screened in on the fourth side for protection from insects and feature four sleeping platforms (bunks without mattresses), a table and benches. They are located at three convenient places for backpackers to overnight: halfway along Lake Superior Trail near Lone Rock, the junction of Correction Line and Big Carp River Trail, and halfway along the Government Peak Trail. There is no additional fee for staying in one, but they are used on a first-come, first-serve basis and can not be reserved in advance. As might be expected, the shelters are heavily used during the summer, and backpackers should still always pack along a tent. You simply cannot count on getting a bunk in one of the shelters.

Fifty backcountry campsites are also scattered throughout the park and in many cases include fire rings bear poles and open-air vault toilets. A dozen of the sites are along the Lake Superior Trail with seven more on the shores of Mirror Lake, five on Lake of the Clouds and 10 stretched along the Little Carp River Trail. They are also used on a first-come, first serve basis and, because of their close proximity to these major features of the park, are the choice of many looking for a place to pitch their tents. On the maps the location and number of sites are denoted with this symbol: ⚑

Finally trailside camping is permitted throughout the park, except within a quarter mile of any cabin, Adirondack shelter, scenic area such as an inland lake or waterfall or road. Nor do you want to actually pitch a tent on the side of the trail. Keep your camps discreet and unobtrusive, and be sure when you depart that the area looks as if you were never there to begin with.

Many of the rivers in the Porkies have bridges, many do not.

🔥 Backcountry Needs

The Porkies are rugged. If you're planning to travel or overnight in the backcountry prepare for them as you would any wilderness. Arrive with the gear you will need to be comfortable, but realize that this is one place where you do not want to be hauling around a 50 or 60-pound pack.

Hiking Boots: Flimsy tennis shoes or running shoes will not do for hiking in the Porkies. There are ridges to climb, roots to stumble over, and rocks to traverse. For these kind of conditions you need a pair of good, well-designed hiking boots. The ultralight nylon and leather boots that dominate the market today provide excellent foot protection for any trek in the park. Just make sure you toss an extra pair of wool socks into your pack along with a first aid kit for feet (moleskin, bandages, blister cream).

Stove: Camp fires in the park are limited to designated fire rings, making a lightweight backpacking stove, such as a the Whisperlite from MSR, a necessity. Whether you plan to rent a cabin or pitch a tent, do all your cooking on a small stove. It will make meal preparation a lot easier and faster. You will soon discover down wood is a scarce item in many popular backcountry areas. The desire for nightly campfires literally strips the surrounding woods of fallen timber before the summer is over.

Clothes: If you are arriving during the summer, come prepared for cool, wet weather. Then when the sun breaks out and the temperatures hit 80 degrees, you won't mind lugging around the extra clothes. Even in the middle of the summer, the nights can be cool, and the wind off Lake Superior can rip right through you. If you're planning a backpacking adventure or extensive dayhiking, make sure you pack along rain gear, preferably both parka and pants. On overnight treks, you should also have an insulating layer, a wool sweater or better still a synthetic pile jersey such as the Patagonia Synchilla, for those all-day rainstorms or a sudden drop in the temperature. For trips to the park in spring and fall, you need even more protection against wet and cold weather, including wool

A downhill skier heads towards the park's Chalet.

hat, mittens and even lightweight polypropylene underwear.

Tent: A tent in the backcountry serves two purposes; keeping you dry inside and keeping the bugs outside. Make sure your unit has a rain-fly and a bug-proof netting. Pack along a quality sleeping pad to place under your sleeping bag, and you shouldn't have any problem getting a good sleep at night.

Water: All water taken from the rivers and lakes, even Lake Superior, should either be boiled for three minutes or run through a water filter system designed to remove the cyst, Giardia lamblia. That means packing a reliable filter system or enough gas to boil water every day. Drinking water is available at Union Bay or Presque Isle campgrounds.

Other Equipment: Bugs are a fact of life in any wilderness area. Bring an insect repellent, especially in June and July, and still pray for a steady wind off Lake Superior. Every hiking party should have a map and compass and the knowledge to use them correctly. The park is covered by three USGS topographical sections (scale 1:62,500); *Thomaston, White Pine* and *Carp River.* The Visitor Center also sells a map that covers the elevation and trails of the entire park that is much more updated but lacks the detail of USGS topos.

❄ When To Go

The park is open year-round and the frost-free period is from June to September. Not surprising, that is also when most visitors arrive in the park, especially from late June through mid-August.

Do insects horrify you? Keep in mind that the U.P. has a black fly season from mid-May through mid-June and many feel that this insect is by far the most irritant one in the backcountry. After black flies you are left to deal with mosquitoes, deer flies, an occasional swarm of no-see-ums, gnats, and other assorted species. By mid-August the number of insects begins to taper down and by early September they are rarely noticed.

In my opinion, the ideal time to visit the park is in September. Fall colors peak around the third week of the month and are spectacular at this park. There is no worry about bugs and the summer rush of hikers has long since left the campgrounds and backcountry. If you are looking for what many refer to as a "wilderness experience" (four days without a Big Mac), September through mid-October is the best time to look for it in the Porkies.

Deer hunters move in on Nov. 15 for the 16-day firearm hunt and the winter season generally begins by mid-December though a good snowfall in November is not uncommon. Both downhill and Nordic skiing traditionally last through the month of March.

🐻 Bears

Bears are encountered in the park though not nearly as often as most visitors expect. The reality is that the vast majority of

A black bear eating grass in the spring.

hikers and backpackers never see a bruin during their stay in the Porkies. Because of their keen sense of smell, most bears would only visit a camp if attracted by the odor of food or some other attractive scent.

Thus a little common sense will prevent any problem with bears, and that begins with never feeding a bear nor cooking in or around your tent. Do not store food or scented items such as toothpaste in your tent at night. Pack all food in zip-lock style bags, and then "cache" them at night by hanging them in the bear poles that have been erected at many backcountry campsites. The metal poles are two inches in diameter and 15 feet high. A long rod is provided to hang packs and food on hooks at the top of the pole.

If you are not at a campsite or there is no a bear pole then suspend your food between two trees 25 to 30 feet off the ground and at least 100 feet away from your camp. Remember if you can reach the cache, so can most bears. Roadside campers should wash dishes immediately after a meal and then store food in airtight containers in the trunk of the car.

If you do encounter a bear, keep calm and retreat slowly. Never approach a bear cub, the sow is almost always nearby. Don't close in on a bear with camera in hand.

Loving The Porkies To Death

We love the Porkies so much, one ranger told me, we're slowly killing them. And in a way it's true. If we're not conscious of our behavior in the backcountry, the pristine streams and forests that draws us to this remote corner of Michigan will be lost.

The park is fragile, as is all wilderness, and the only way it will survive the thousands that hike and camp here is if we all practice "low impact use" of the area:

• Pack out all trash, you will find trash containers at the trailheads and in campgrounds. Don't leave trash in the cabins or the shelters, the cost of removing it is astronomical. Don't bury refuse. Animals will dig it up and spread it over a large area. Not only pack out your own trash but go a step further. Pick up and carry out the litter someone else thoughtlessly dropped.

• Build campfires only in designated areas and no fires whatsoever during dry weather when there is a high fire danger alert. Burn only down wood and never cut live trees.

• Do not use motorized methods of transportation or mountain bikes on park trails.

• Do not shortcut switchbacks, start new trails or widen trails when they are wet and muddy. Acccept the inevitable: hiking through the mud is part of the backcountry experience and march on.

• Do not wash or throw wastewater into or close to any water source, stream or lake.

• In the backcountry, bury human waste and tissue paper at least six inches deep.

• Leave the radios and tape recorders at home while visiting the Porkies. The solitude of nature is too rare and valuable to disturb with man-made music.

• And most important, when you break camp, leave no trace of yourself.

3 Campgrounds And Cabins

I'm not a woodsmen, nor a person who really gets close to nature. Roughing it to me is staying at the Holiday Inn when I had reservations at the Hilton.

From the The log book in the Big Carp River Six-Bunk Cabin.

Spending a night in the Porkies? At one time there was a push by some to build a luxurious hotel here, primarily to attract more skiers to the state-managed slopes. It has yet to be built but that's not to say the Porkies doesn't have a wide range of lodging possibilities.

Accommodations int the park are rustic, maybe too rustic for some visitors, but no matter where you unroll your sleeping bag in Michigan it's hard to beat the setting that surrounds you in the Porkies. The two main campgrounds are along Lake Superior, others are situated on small rugged rivers while many of the 16 cabins can be found near waterfalls, overlooking the Great Lake, even on the shores of Lake of the Clouds.

You can sleep on a mattress in a bunk, on a wooden platform in a three-sided shelter or in your 30-foot recreational vehicle in a campground with warm showers, flush toilets, and an electrical outlet to plug in the microwave oven. Regardless where you make camp, spending a night or two in the park greatly enhances any visit, especially if you can escape into the backcountry. But plan ahead as to where you want to stay and then make reservations if they are needed. You don't want to be left out in the cold when night falls on the Porkies.

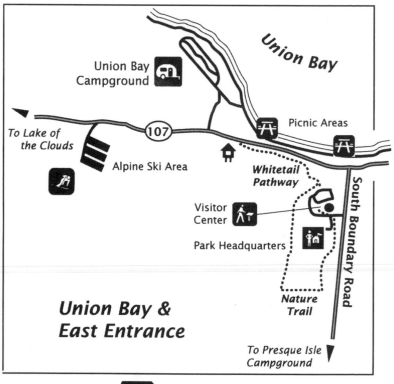

**Union Bay &
East Entrance**

 Campgrounds

There are six campgrounds accessible from the road and annually they host more than 100,000 visitors. Reservations can be made in advance at the two largest, Union Bay and Presque Isle. You can begin reserving sites on the first business day of January for that year by calling the park headquarters at (906) 885-5275.

Sites booked in advance require a small reservation fee as well as a nightly site fee and can be paid either by mailing a check or with a Master or Visa credit card over the phone. In the future, the Parks Division also plans to install a central reservation number for all the state park campgrounds, but you will always be able to reserve a site by directly contacting the park headquarters.

The other four campgrounds are used on a first-come, first-serve basis. Three of them, White Pine Extension, Lost Creek and Union River Outpost, are small, rustic facilities and, the fourth is an organization campground designed for large groups.

Union Bay: This is the largest campground with 99 sites and is the only modern one in the park. Located on the east side, Union Bay is reached from M-107, just beyond South Boundary Road, and consists of a grassy shelf overlooking Lake Superior with little shade. The facilities include showers, modern restrooms, a sanitation station for RVs along with a improved boat launch on Lake Superior. Nearby the Whitetail Path departs along M-107 to the Visitor's Center a mile away.

Union Bay fills daily for two weeks from late July through mid-August. During the rest of the summer it is likely to be full five out of seven days. There are usually plenty of open sites before mid-June and beginning in September. The restrooms and showers are operated from mid-May through the third week in October.

Presque Isle: On the west end of the park is Presque Isle Campground, a semi-modern facility with 88 sites located on a bluff above Lake Superior near the picturesque mouth of its namesake river. The campground can be reached by either following South Boundary Road around the park or from US-2 by heading 17 miles north from Wakefield on County Road 519 to its end.

Sites are scattered around two loops, and a dozen of them are on the edge of the bluff overlooking the lake. The rest are in a large grassy area, shaded by a scattering of large maples while the campground itself is surrounded by woods. Facilities include tables, fire rings, showers and modern restrooms, and a sanitation station but not electric outlets.

The lack of electricity for RVers is the reason, no doubt, why Presque Isle doesn't fill to capacity as often as Union Bay. In late July to early August the campground fills two or three nights per week and occasionally during the rest of the summer. Those planning to camp at Presque Isle should keep in mind the nearest gasoline station and store are 17 miles away in Wakefield.

Union River Outpost: A mile south of the Visitor Center is this three-site rustic campground that is due to be renovated in the near future. Overlooking the Union River, the sites are in a stand of hardwoods and pine and well secluded from South Boundary Road. Unfortunately, Union River could be filled any night of the summer due to it close proximity to M-107. Facilities include vault toilets, fire rings, and tables, but there is no hand pump or any other safe water source. Nearby is the posted trailheads for Union Mine Trail and Union Spring Trail that leads into the interior of the Porkies.

Lost Creek: Located 7 miles along South Boundary Road is Lost Creek Campground. The facility is situated across the road from the trailhead of the Lost Lake Trail and has three semi-open sites near Lost Creek, but not directly on it. There are fire rings, tables and vault toilets but no source of safe water.

White Pine Extension: Continuing west along South Boundary Road, White Pine Extension is reached in 10 miles from M-107 and is the least likely to be filled of the three outlying campgrounds. The outpost campground lies near the Little Iron River and features eight sites in a wooded area. Like the others, White Pine has tables, fire rings and vault toilets but no water source. The nearest trailheads are on the Summit Peak access road 1.5 miles west on South Boundary Road.

Organization Campground: Located off M-107, just east of South Boundary Road, is an organization campground for groups. There are no minimum requirements for the number of people in a group, and it is used on a first-come, first-serve basis. The facility consists of two group sites, each capable of holding roughly 25 people. There are vault toilets and tables but no source of water. Water can be obtained at Union Bay Campground. Interested groups should call the park headquarters in advance of their trip for more information.

 # Cabins

Perhaps one of the most unique aspects of Porcupine Mountains Wilderness State Parks is its trailside cabins. Other parks

Buckshot Landing Cabin on the shores of Lake Superior.

have cabins, even some you have to hike into, but none have as many that are accessed from such an extensive network of foot trails as does the Porkies. This may be the only place in the Midwest where you can put together a legitimate three or four-day backpacking trip with every night spent in a different cabin rather than a tent.

The cabins range in size from two to eight bunks and access could be a five minute walk from the road or a four-mile trek. The units are rented from May through the firearm deer season which runs from Nov. 16-30. Three of them, however, are especially built for winter use and are rented out year-round (see chapter 9).

Facilities include bunks with mattresses, wood-burning stove, table, chairs, pots and pans, plates and eating utensils, saw and axe. There is also a log book in each cabin that makes for some entertaining reading. Cabin users should bring sleeping bags or other bedding, food, towels, either a lantern or candles for lighting, dish soap, and toilet paper. A small backcountry stove is also highly recommend for cooking as preparing meals on the wood stoves takes a great deal more time and down wood can be scarce during the summer in some areas. You will need to either boil or filter your water for drinking or cooking purposes as there are no hand pumps in the backcountry.

Some cabin users rent one unit and then use it as a base for dayhikes deeper into the backcountry. But the majority of people, say park officials, rent several cabins and then spend their visit hiking from one to the next. All of this, of course, requires careful planning and advance reservations.

You can begin reserving cabins on the first business day of January for the following year. In other words, you could book a cabin in January of 1995 for use in 1996 and if you have particular dates and certain cabins, you may want to do that. If you can be somewhat flexible in your dates and cabin selection, however, chances are good if you call four to six months in advance the park staff can find a unit for you.

Finally there are always cancellations, even last minutes ones, and during the summer a cabin vacancy list is posted each morning in the Visitors Center with whatever is open that night...if any of them are. In the end, it's a rare night in the Porkies for any cabin to be empty.

Buckshot Landing: This four-bunk is a scenic 2.5 mile hike in from the Lake Superior trailhead on M-107...and a steep hike back out as you have to climb from lake level back up the Escarpment. The cabin is situated just off the shoreline, 30 yards from the water, and it north windows provide a view of the lake itself. A day can be spent hiking Lake Superior to the shelter near Lone Rock while the sunsets on a clear evening are spectacular anywhere along the shoreline.

Big Carp River Six Bunk: This is one of the largest and most scenic cabins in the park, with one row of windows overlooking Lake Superior and another with a view of the Big Carp River. It's a 5.5-mile trek from Buckshot Landing, but the quickest way to reach it is to begin on the Pinkerton Trail off of South Boundary Road, which is still a walk of 4 miles. Outside a bench overlooks a bridge and a large pool in the river where more than one person

The Lake of the Clouds Cabin at the base of the Escarpment.

has enjoyed his morning coffee. The mouth of the Big Carp River is a busy place on a summer evening, however, due to a trailside campground and two other cabins in the area.

Big Carp River Four Bunk: Up the river and slightly more secluded is this four bunk unit on a bluff along the west bank. It is near the start of the Cross Trail and is situated directly above some deep pools where salmon can be seen gathering in the fall.

Lake Superior: The third cabin at the mouth is a four-bunk unit on the west side of the river just west along the Lake Superior Trail. This cabin is more shrouded in trees and lacks the clear view of Lake Superior or Big Carp River which makes the other two so popular. All three are the furthest from a trailhead of any in the park, a 4-mile hike along the Pinkerton and Lake Superior Trails.

Little Carp: Perched on a steep hill above the mouth of the river is this four-bunk cabin. Little Carp is a mile west of the Big Carp River and 3 miles from South Boundary Road at the end of the Pinkerton Trail. With a full pack on, the hill can be a scramble at times, especially in the rain. Once at the cabin you're greeted with a partial view of the river below but none of Lake Superior through the surrounding trees.

Speakers: This four-bunk cabin is located near the junction between the Lake Superior Trail and Speakers Trail. It is a rugged 2.5-mile hike in from Presque Isle Campground or a fairly easy mile from South Boundary Road. A newer cabin that was built in 1977, Speakers has a scenic setting as it is situated on the edge of a bluff overlooking both the Great Lake and the mouth of Speakers Creek. Outside you'll find a fire ring and benches positioned to take advantage of the view. Nearby by is sandy stretch of shoreline for those brave enough to take a diip in frigid Lake Superior.

Greenstone Falls: Built in 1948 and renovated after a fire in 1990, Greenstone Falls is a four-bunk cabin that overlooks Little Carp River while its namesake cascade is just upstream. The cabin is 5.5 miles from Mirror Lake, 6.4 miles from the mouth of the Big Carp River, via the Little Carp River Trail, or an easy mile walk from the end of Little Carp River Road off South Boundary Road. The only drawback of the unit is its location right on Little Carp River Trail, a popular route during the summer.

Section 17: One of the most secluded cabins in the park, Section 17 is a four-bunk unit on the south side of Little Carp River, just across where Cross Trail joins Little Carp River Trail. It is 5.5 miles up the Little Carp River Trail from Lake Superior or 1.5 miles if you follow the spur off of South Boundary. Originally built as a ranger patrol cabin, Section 17 sits on a low bluff overlooking the river in a stand of hardwoods whose colors are stunning in the late September. A half mile upstream is the Greenstone Falls.

Lily Pond: Another four-bunk cabin off by itself in a somewhat secluded location in the park. Lily Pond faces a foot bridge over

Section 17 Cabin along the Little Carp River Trail.

Little Carp River and the pond that it flows through for a scenic setting. There is a canoe that can be used in the small lake though fishing is marginal at best. The cabin lies on the Little Carp River Trail but the quickest route to it is a 3-mile hike along Lily Pond Trail from Summit Peak Road.

Mirror Lake Eight Bunk: The classic log cabin in the wilderness and the first to be built in the park. This eight-bunk unit reminds most users of a hunting lodge in the mountains both for its size and it's perch above the lake. It is roomy inside, while outside there is a bench where sunrise over Mirror Lake can be enjoyed. The cabin also comes with two rowboats for use on the lake. The only draw back is North Mirror Lake Trail which runs right past the front door. Envious backpackers are forever peeking inside. The cabin is a rugged 4-mile trek from the Lake of the Clouds Escarpment or a shorter and slightly easier 2.5-mile hike from Summit Peak Road on South Mirror Lake Trail.

Mirror Lake Four Bunk: Just to the west is this four-bunk cabin, the second of three units on the north shore of the lake. The log structure is not perched on the edge of the lake like the eight-bunk unit, but still has a view of the shoreline and is equipped with a rowboat. The North Mirror Lake Trail also runs in front of the cabin.

Mirror Lake Two-Bunk: The third cabin on Mirror Lake is actually positioned above the water on a ridge, away from hikers passing through. Mirror Lake Two-Bunk is another ranger cabin converted for renting and the smallest in the park. It's a tight squeeze for even two people, thus its nickname; *the Honeymoon Suite*. But it's location is a much more secluded spot to spend the evening even if you do have to scramble down the slope to enjoy the lake. A canoe is provided with the unit so it is easier to haul it up and down.

Lake of the Clouds: This is a four-bunk cabin situated only a few feet from the shore of the park's most noted natural treasure. Hardwoods surround the unit but from its windows and bench there is a clear view of the water and the ridges that enclose it. Lake of the Clouds is a hike of less than a mile from the Escarpment viewing area along the North Mirror Lake Trail, but a steep climb back out. The cabin comes with a boat and, needless to say, is an extremely popular unit.

Union River: This eight-bunk cabin is one of three new "winter units", the reason for the cement floor, but it is still a charmer. It's located off the Union Spring Trail, a mile from the trailhead, and overlooks a spot where the Union River swirls past a rocky bluff. The cabin features a wide L-shape kitchen. Because it's insulated for winter the room warms up fast once the stove is lit and stays warm throughout the night.

Whitetail: The second winter unit is located on Lake Superior and is accessed from Deer Yard Trail, primarily a cross country ski

Mirror Lake Eight-Bunk Cabin, your own mountain lodge in the middle of the Porkies.

route. It's a mile hike-in from the trailhead just west of the downhill ski area on M-107. The design is similar to Union River, but Whitetail, an eight-bunk cabin, is on a bluff overlooking Lake Superior in a forest of young hardwoods and paper birch. The view is excellent and the picnic table and fire pit are angled to take full advantage of the watery horizon.

Gitche Gumee: This cabin was built for both winter use and physically impaired visitors. It is on the south side of M-107 before South Boundary Road. The trail to Gitchee Gumee, a five-minute walk from where you park the car, is handicapped accessible as is the vault toilet outside. There are no other foot trails nearby.

Fly fisherman with a steelhead.

4 Wilderness Fishing

Twang!

Graphite, in the form of a six-foot rod strapped to my backpack, met green wood in the form of a young beech sapling and for a split second they were intertwined with each other. But my next step separated this composite and wooden arch in the middle the trail, leaving them both vibrating and me cursing under my breath.

Why didn't I take the time to find my four-piece, trail rod?

No salmon trip ever began like this for me. Not only was I hiking to the river, as opposed to driving, but I was carrying a 40-pound backpack so I could spend a few nights deep inside Porcupine Mountains Wilderness State Park. Then there was the tip of my rod, getting mixed up in every branch along the narrow trail.

Twang!

All this to reach the Big Carp, a river few fishermen think of when the annual spawning runs of Chinook and coho are heating up in Great Lakes tributaries. That's because you tend to twang your rods hiking in. Yet the run up the Big Carp offers something no other river in the state can do in the fall; the opportunity to catch salmon and later steelhead in the state's most scenic setting. To fish a pool without being elbow to elbow with 20 other anglers along the bank. To fish all day and not see a single driftboat.

To catch a salmon in the solitude of the wilderness.

Although rarely considered an angler's final destination, there are fishing opportunities throughout the Porkies. When you visit, by all means, pack a rod; but also be aware of the limitations that a wilderness imposes on anglers. And that begins with the realization that most of the park's fishing opportunities are hike-in experiences.

The park does maintain an improved boat launch in the Union Bay campground, and anglers use it to troll the deep water fishery of Lake Superior. Lake trout is the most predominate species caught and the waters just a few miles off the park offer some of the best lake trout fishing in the area, especially in June and July. Anglers also troll for steelhead, salmon, and brown trout.

All fishing beyond that, however, is done in a backcountry setting which includes a ban on outboard or electric motors, even if you have a back strong enough to carry one in. Fishing the handful of lakes within the park from shore can be rewarding, but also somewhat restrictive due to the lack of shoreline trail. If your sole desire is to fish, either pack in waders or better yet, carry in a boat. Some cabins come with a rowboat (see chapter three) while a canoe can be portaged into Lake of the Clouds. To fish any of the other three, your best bet is a belly boat as none of the lakes are so large they can't be covered in a float tube.

Seasons, tackle regulations and limits that apply to the rest of Michigan, are in effect in the state park. All anglers over the age of 12 must purchase a Michigan fishing license. Here is a brief overview of the fishing opportunities in the Porkies:

Lake of the Clouds: The 300-acre lake has a maximum depth of 15 feet. Lake of the Clouds is the largest in the park and probably the most photographed lake anywhere. But in all this scenic splendor what is often overlooked is the lake's outstanding smallmouth bass fishery. Most bass range from 13 to 16 inches though an occasional 20-inch, five-pound bass is hooked. Anglers work a variety of rigs (jigs with twister tails, countdown crankbaits and Mepps spinners) bouncing them along rocky drop-offs on the north side of the lake or running them pass deadheads and old beaver lodges near the shore. Generally live bait, such as nightcrawlers on a harness, are by far the most productive.

Lake of the Clouds is a mile descent from the Escarpment Overlook parking lot at the end of M-107 and close enough to justify hauling a canoe in for a day. Just remember it's a steep climb

Anglers use the cabin rowboat to fish Lake of the Clouds.

out. The four-bunk cabin on the lake's north shore also has a rowboat. Catch and release is strongly recommended throughout the park but especially in Lake of the Clouds.

Mirror Lake: This 83-acre lake has a maximum depth of 40 feet and is stocked every other year with brook trout, The hatchery-raised trout range from six to eight inches in length and at that size have an excellent survival rate. At times, especially in the spring, the fishing can be excellent in Mirror lake. But because of three cabins and the backcountry campsites, the lake experiences the heaviest fishing pressure in the park.

The lake is a 2.5 to 4-mile hike in depending on which trailhead you depart from. All three cabins on the lake are equipped with a boat, the Mirror Lake Eight-Bunk Cabin with two boats.

Lily Pond: This small lake in the southwest corner of the park is has a surface of 12 acres and a depth of 11 feet. Lily Pond is not stocked but the streams and creeks that feed it contain natural brook trout that migrate into Lily Pond. The lake is a 3-mile hike in and there is a rowboat at the cabin.

Lost Lake: Situated in the southeast corner of the park is Lost Lake, the smallest of the lakes and a 2-mile walk in from its trailhead on South Boundary Road. The lake is not stocked and receives little if any fishing pressure during the summer.

Union River Impoundment: This impoundment of Union Spring was traditionally stocked with brook trout and at one time supported a good fishery. Gradually it has filled in with silt, the curse of most impoundments, and is no longer stocked. Today the fishing is generally poor. The impoundment is reached after a 1.5-mile hike from South Boundary Road, and there are backcountry campsites near it.

Big Carp River: Unquestionably the most remote river in the park, this river is probably also the most difficult to reach salmon run in the state. Beginning near Lake of the Clouds, the Big Carp flows entirely in the Porcupine Mountains, miles from any road. Several trails lead to its mouth, but the shortest hike in is still a 4-mile trek via the Pinkerton and Lake Superior trails.

Salmon begin appearing in mid-September and peak by early October when, as one park manager put it, "Some pools are so loaded you can practically walk across them." In streams, salmon are taken on spinners, spoons, plugs, spawn, even flies, and single eggs with rods and six-pound test line.

April is the prime month for taking a spring steelhead in the park though in recent years the runs have been poor. These are wild steelhead as the rivers are not planted and occasionally the fish range from four to six pounds. Anglers turn to #2 Mepps spinners as well as spawn while fly fishermen have an excellent opportunity to use nymphs and attractors on the Big Carp to hook into the spawning trout.

The river can be easily waded as most of its lower portion consists of pools and rapids with good stretches of gravel in between. The upper portion of the Big Carp, above Correction Line Trail, hass some of the best brook trout waters in the park

Fishing In The Porkies

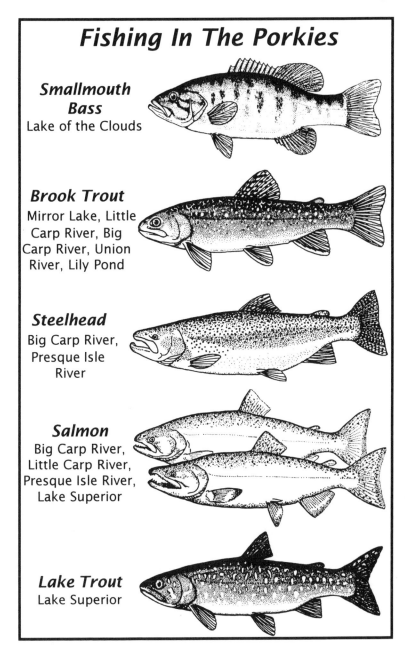

Smallmouth Bass
Lake of the Clouds

Brook Trout
Mirror Lake, Little Carp River, Big Carp River, Union River, Lily Pond

Steelhead
Big Carp River, Presque Isle River

Salmon
Big Carp River, Little Carp River, Presque Isle River, Lake Superior

Lake Trout
Lake Superior

Surf fisherman casting for brown trout and steelhead in the spring.

but be prepared to buck a lot brush to reach the desirable pools.

Little Carp River: It may be labeled a river on the map but the Little Carp is more like a mountain steam in many places. This river also attracts a steelhead run in the spring with anglers catching fish that range up to four pounds. Further up stream the Little Carp has pools and pockets of brook trout. Overall it is fished much harder than the Big Carp due to its proximity to South Boundary Road. It is a 3-mile hike to the river mouth along the Pinkerton Trail although the better brook trout section, near Greenstone Falls, is only a mile hike in.

Presque Isle River: This spectacular river on the west side of the park receives the most attention from steelheaders, but its run is short as Manabezho Falls stop the trout from moving further up stream. Most anglers arrive to surf fish the river mouth where they spike their rods into the ground and work rigs of cut spawn or spoons.

Further up river, beyond South Boundary Road, there is a brook trout fishery to enjoy. The river mouth is a short descent from the Presque Isle picnic area at the end of County Road 519. To reach the best brook trout pools, you are on your own through brush, though the county road parallels it closely in the beginning.

Other Streams: The Union River has a steelhead run of its own in the spring and parts of the river can be reached by the ski trail that parallels it after crossing South Boundary Road. Upper portions of it can be fished for brook trout.

Naturally the best brook trout fishing in the park is in the hardest spots to reach. You can spend an adventurous afternoon bushwhacking up the more remote streams searching for that hidden pool with a 12-inch brookie. Good streams to search include the Upper Carp River which can be accessed 2.5 miles up Lost Lake Trail or Little Iron River that flows near White Pine Extension and Lost Creek outpost campgrounds.

Union Bay: Fishing can also be very good in Union Bay during the spring and fall both for surf anglers and those with a boat set up for trolling. Anglers tend to target lake trout and salmon in the fall and steelhead and brown trout in the spring. Anglers trolling spoons along the shoreline on planer boards do especially well with brown trout in the spring.

A hiker enjoys the Greenstone Falls, one of many along the Little Carp River. Porcupine Mountains boasts more waterfalls than any other state park in Michigan. Within the park are some of the largest cascades in the Midwest.

5 The Waterfalls

She stopped along the Big Carp River at the end of a long day that began by shouldering her 35-pound backpack at the Lake of the Clouds Overlook. Now she figured she was only a mile or so from her destination on Lake Superior when she noticed the sign.

It read "Bathtub Falls."

She looked around and missed it at first. Not surprising. The second half of Big Carp River Trail is a pathway of cascades from thundering Shining Cloud Falls to many that are unnamed but still delightful drops in the current. Bathtub Falls was not like any of them. It is was little more than a splash in the river's whitewater run to the Great Lake.

Then she noticed the pools and flat boulders nearby, and suddenly her feet were aching from miles of rugged trail and her shoulders were throbbing from a backpack with too much gear. She dropped the pack, untied her boots, and stripped off two pairs of socks. Her feet were free at last, and she eased them into the swirling cold water of the river.

Ahhhhh! A jacuzzi in the middlle of the wilderness! She lay back on the warm rock, stared at the blue sky above her and thought "nicest falls I've seen all day."

Some places in Michigan might have bigger and more impressive waterfalls, but no state park can boast a larger collection of cascades than the Porcupine Mountains. Within the park there are more than a dozen named falls, numerous others that aren't and after any hard rain there will be falling water in every creek and stream. Most of the cascades are only in the backcountry and can only be enjoyed by those who leave their cars and take to the trails on foot.

Waterfall lovers, intent on seeing as many as possible, would do well to include in their intinerary the Big Carp River Trail, Little Carp River Trail and the East-West River Trails along the Presque Isle. What follows is a thumbnail stretch of the major falls in the parks. Some are spectacular and labeled on every map while the beauty of others is seen only by those with aching feet and throbbing shoulders.

Manabezho Falls: There are four named cascades on Presque Isle River within the park, and three of them can be viewed by hiking the East or West River Trail. The swing bridge near the Presque Isle picnic area provides an excellent view of the river's final drop into Lake Superior where the spinning action of the current is so strong it has carved half circles in the bed rock and along the shoreline.

Following the West Trail boardwalk upriver, you reach Manabezho Falls in about 200 yards, the most impressive section of whitewater in the Presque Isle. Here the 150-foot-wide river drops more than 20 feet over a rock ledge in a thunder of copper color water and mist.

Manido Falls: Another 100 yards upriver is Manido Falls, which drops a total of 25 feet; first over a series of declining rock steps then a ledge where the water slides over large sections of shale. The falls can be seen from both sides of the river but farther along West Trail there is an observation platform extending from the riverbank.

Nawadaha Falls: Closest to South Boundary Road is Nawadaha Falls, a cascade that drops 15 feet over a series rock steps. The falls are easier to see from the East Trail than the west side where you need to leave the path to get a good look at it.

Overlooked Falls: There are five named falls along the Little Carp River with the first two reached in less than a mile from the end of Little Carp River Road. Overlooked is a mere 100 feet from where you park the car, and it's actually a pair of cascades with a total drop 10 feet, with the second falls split in the middle by a huge rock boulder.

Greenstone Falls: Several more small falls are passed along

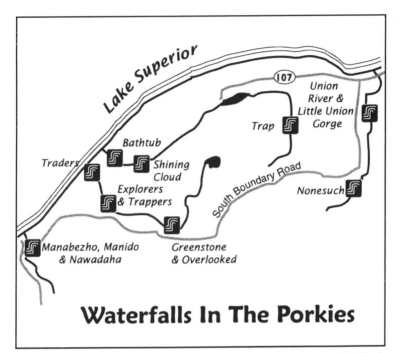

Waterfalls In The Porkies

the trail and then 0.75 mile from the trailhead, just along the Little Carp River Trail toward the cabins, you reach Greenstone Falls. Set in a small gorge, the cascade features a 15-foot wide veil that tumbles six feet down a series of rock steps and small boulders.

Explorers and Trappers Falls: This pair of falls is located close together along the Little Carp River Trail, 4 miles from Little Carp Road or 2.5 miles from the trailhead along Lake Superior. If heading towards the lake, you pass Trappers first then ford the river to quickly arrive at Explorers, a more distinct cascade. Here the 12-foot wide Little Carp River forms a veil as it tumbles over a rock enbankment.

Traders Falls: The final falls are a half mile from the Lake Superior shoreline. The Little Carp River departs along the east side bank, opposite the cabin, and immediately climbs a gorge. You can see Traders Falls just before the trail descends to the river bank.

Shining Cloud Falls: In the northern half of the Big Carp River Trail, after its junction with Correction Line Trail, you pass almost a dozen waterfalls beginning with one of the most impressive cascades in the park. Shining Cloud is also the highest in the Porkies at almost 800 feet and reached 1.5 miles from the Lake Superior Trailhead or 7.5 miles from the Lake of the Clouds Overlook. The cascade is set in a deep, rocky gorge and is a 30 to 35-foot drop split by a large rocky outcropping before spilling into a large pool.

Bathtub Falls: From Shining Cloud north along the river you pass a dozen cascades, all unnamed but several have a drop of six feet or more with inviting pools at their base. This magnificent stretch of whitewater, where the Big Carp River tumbles down to the lower level of Lake Superior, ends with Bathtub Falls, a series of small ledges and little pools.

Trap Falls: The best cascade in the east half of the Park is Trap Falls. These can be reached at 2.5 miles on the Government Peak Trail from M-107 or 4.5 miles if you begin on the Union Spring Trail. Situated in an impressive gorge area, the falls feature a 15 to 20-foot drop along a narrow rock slide and end in the most inviting pool in the park. The area is shaded by towering pines and there's bench overlooking the river to rest your feet and enjoy this scenic spot.

Little Union Gorge And Union River Falls: There are several small falls in the Little Union Gorge area and along the Union River that can be accessed from the Union Mine Trail. You have to leave the trail to see the most impressive cascades along the Union River. They are best reached from the iron bridge at Union River Outpost Campground. From the center of the bridge, you can see small falls upstream while a ski\mountain bike trail will take you along the river downstream to view additional drops in the river. The falls on the Little Union River can be very impressive in the spring runoff or after a heavy rain. Most of them can be viewed from the trail.

Nonesuch Falls: Located on the Little Iron River near the remains Nonesuch Mine is this 12-foot cascade that is divided by

Enjoying the whitewater of the Big Carp River.

a boulder in the middle. It ends with a seven-foot deep pool before the river continues it journey to Lake Superior. The falls are reached from South Boundary Road 4.3 miles south of M-107. Where South Boundary makes a sharp curve west, the gravel road continues south and in less than a mile reaches the cascade.

Backpackers take a well deserved break in the Porkies. The Lake Superior Trail is a favorite overnight adventure into the park for many visitors.

6 Lake Superior Trail

The longest route in the Porkies is the Lake Superior Trail, a 16-mile walk from M-107 to the Presque Isle day-use area. This is one of Michigan's best known footpaths, an extended hike that ranks in popularity with the Greenstone Trail on Isle Royale and the Lakeshore Trail in Pictured Rocks National Lakeshore.

The Lake Superior Trail takes you from one side of the state park to the other, winding along the largest body of freshwater in the world and crossing such scenic rivers as the Big Carp, Little Carp and Presque Isle. It is an avenue through the most remote corner of park's 60,000 acres and provides access to six trailside cabins, two backcountry campsite areas, and a three-sided shelter.

This trail allows you to witness Lake Superior's fury on a stormy day or a stunning sunset of oranges and reds when the lake is calm. Hiked in its entirety, the Lake Superior route can leave you with that special sense of having trekked from one corner of the park to the other.

Ironically, few people experience the trail from end to end. Being a point-to-point route, there is a logistical problem of getting back to a car for any party of hikers who do not arrive in two or more vehicles. On Isle Royale there is a ferry or a float plane that will return you to your starting point. At Pictured Rocks there is a van service. In the Porkies, you are simply stuck 25 miles away, via South Boundary Road, from a vehicle at the trailhead. For this reason most trekkers combine a portion of the Lake Superior Trail with others to form a loop within the park.

The most common itinerary is to begin at M-107 and to return along Carp River Trail, a three-day, 18-mile hike. A slightly longer version would be to include Correction Line and North Mirror Lake trails, a 20-mile trek. Perhaps the longest backpack in the park is to return along Little Carp River, Government Peak and Escarpment trails, a 5-day, 32-mile walk.

To make the following description as useful to the most people as possible, Lake Superior Trail will be outlined from the M-107 trailhead to Big Carp River and then from the Presque Isle trailhead to Big Carp River. The easiest direction to hike is east to west due to the fact that you begin on the Escarpment instead of having to climb it at the end.

Although it never climbs into the ridges that are technically the Porcupine Mountains, the Lake Superior Trail can still be a rugged walk at times, especially the west end where have to you climb in and out of several steep ravines to cross streams. Nor should you expect a view of the Great Lake every step of the way. However, the trail winds close to the lake from the Adirondack shelter to Little Carp River and in this stretch there are many opportunities to stop and admire the water. Otherwise you will find the rest of the trail for the most part is a path through woods.

Like the rest of the park's trail system, after a hard rain the conditions can get muddy, even sloppy at times, and streams can be difficult to cross. Fortunately the Lake Superior Trail is not nearly as bad as others due to a major upgrade of the route that began in 1993 by the park staff which included installing two miles of boardwalk from one end to the other.

Lake Superior Trail

M-107 To Big Carp River
Distance: *2.5 miles to Buckshot Cabin*
6.5 miles to Trailside Shelter
9 miles to Big Carp River
Highest Point: *1,220 feet*
Hiking Time: *5 to 7 hours*

The eastern trailhead to the Lake Superior Trail is posted along M-107, about a mile east from the road's end at the Escarpment Overlook parking area. The trail departs north from

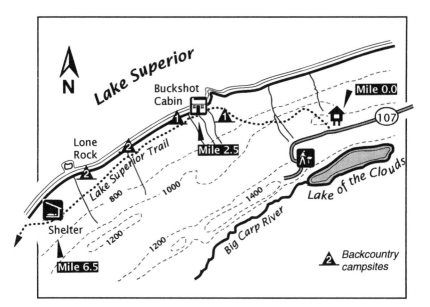

the state road in an old growth forest of pine for a half mile until you gradually ascend to the high point of 1,220 feet and your first view of Lake Superior. From the rocky outcrop you can see Lone Rock just to the west and if the day is clear the Apostle Islands off Wisconsin. This is as high as the trail climbs as you never even break 800 feet in the remaining 15 miles.

The route swings west, follows the ridge briefly to unveil more views of the Great Lake and and split log bench then begins dropping to the shoreline. At first the descent is gentle but then becomes a rapid, knee-bending hike downward when the trail swings more to the north. After a mile, you finally bottom out in an area of young hardwoods. Though you are only a few hundred yards from the lake, it is hard to spot the water through the trees.

The trail swings west, crosses a wet area and within a quarter mile you pass **Buckshot Landing Cabin**, a 2.5 mile walk from M-107. The four-bunk cabin is situated 30 yards from the shoreline with a pleasant view of the lake from its windows. Those who have thoughtfully reserved the unit in advance can throw down the packs and rub your shoulders. Others can choose a **backcountry**

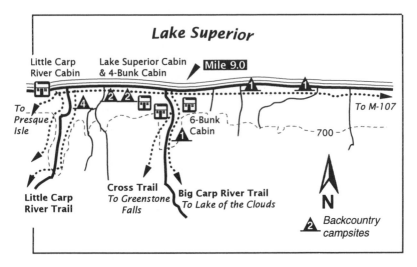

campsite. There is one before the cabin and five more posted on the trail before Lone Rock.

The next 6.5 miles to Big Carp River is one of the most level trails in this unleveled park and by far the easiest stretch of the shoreline route. Beyond the three-sided shelter, is the most scenic section as well. Initially after passing the cabin, the trail dips into the trees, a good 50 yards from the lake, and for the first mile the water remains hidden behind the foliage around you.

Eventually the trail swings closer to the Great Lake in the second mile and often, in the middle of the forest, you can hear the waves crashing along the red pebbled beaches just to the north. Partial views of the lake begin to appear between the trees, especially in the fall, and at 5.5 miles from the trailhead you reach the posted junction to Lone Rock. The spur takes you 20 yards to the lakeshore and the view of the huge boulder lying offshore.

The main trail continues to stay close to the lakeshore for the next mile, but not along it, until it reaches the ***Adirondack shelter*** 6.5 miles from M-107. The small three-sided hut is screened in on its fourth side and features four wooden platforms for sleeping, a table and benches. It is not directly on the water, but a short path leads down to the lake.

A trail junction near the Big Carp River Six-Bunk Cabin.

Those pushing on will find the remaining 2.5 miles to Big Carp River a delightful stretch of the long route. The trail immediately swings towards the lake and from the middle of the path you are rewarded with a continuous view of this sea of blue. The view occurs for most of the walk and often you stroll right along the edge of the shoreline with the waves breaking only a few feet away.

There is not any climbing involved as the trail traverses the narrow bench that lies between the lake and a low ridge that rises 60 feet to the southeast. Stop often and soak your feet in this portion. For many people this is the highpoint of hiking the Lake Superior Trail. Two **backcountry campsites** are passed.

Eventually you break into a large flat area and the **Big Carp Six-Bunk Cabin** on the east side of the river comes into view. The mouth of the Big Carp River is the furthermost point in the park from any road. Break a leg here and it is a *looong* 4 mile trek to pavement. But it is also one of the most scenic places to spend a night.

Just before reaching the river, a junction with the Big Carp

River Trail is reached. By combining a portion of that route with Correction Line Trail you could reach Mirror Lake in 7 miles.

The river is crossed by a wooden foot bridge that lies between two huge boulders with a bench at one end. Here you can sit and rest those tired toes while viewing the river rippling into the surf of Lake Superior and if it is September you can watch salmon spawn upstream. The mouth of the Big Carp River is a large flat of gravel, boulders and large trunks of driftwood trees washed up during one of Lake Superior's moments of fury. This makes an excellent spot to drag out the sleeping pad on a clear evening to watch the sunset.

Once across the bridge you immediately come to the junction with Cross Trail which leads 5 miles to South Boundary Road. Just up the trail is the **Big Carp River Four-Bunk Cabin** in a more secluded spot overlooking a pool in the river.

Continue along Lake Superior Trail for a few yards to reach **Lake Superior Cabin**, a four-bunk unit tucked away in the trees and out of view for the most part from both the river and the lake. A little farther is a stairway that leads up a bluff to the **Big Carp River Campsites** where you will find numbered tent pads and fire rings above the trail.

If you are continuing on the Little Carp River, Cross, or the second half of the Lake Superior Trail, try to squeeze in a side trip to Shining Cloud Falls. It is a one-way trek of 1.2 miles from the mouth with most of the time spent paralleling scenic Big Carp River until you reach the falls, a stunning sight.

Presque Isle Campground To Big Carp River

Distance: *2 miles to Speakers Cabin*
6 miles to Little Carp River
7 miles to Big Carp River
Highest Point: *707 feet*
Hiking Time: *4 to 6 hours*

The highest point along the western half of the Lake Superior Trail is only 707 feet reached near Pinkerton Stream. But don't let

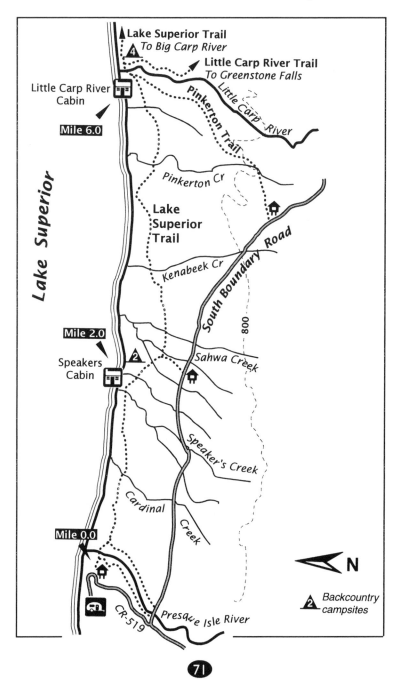

Lake Superior Trail
To Big Carp River

Little Carp River Trail
To Greenstone Falls

Pinkerton Trail

Little Carp River

Little Carp River Cabin

Mile 6.0

Pinkerton Cr

Lake Superior Trail

Lake Superior

Kenabeek Cr

South Boundary Road

800

Mile 2.0

Speakers Cabin

Sahwa Creek

Speaker's Creek

Cardinal Creek

Mile 0.0

Presque Isle River

CR-519

N

Backcountry campsites

that deceive you. You do an awfully lot of climbing, and descending, along this stretch and it begins the minute you depart from the backpacker's parking lot near the Presque Isle Campground.

You no sooner lock your car then you are descending along a boardwalk and stairway towards the Presque Isle River, crossing a stretch of whitewater on an impressive swing bridge. A thin peninsula in the mouth of the river lies on the other side where a spur diverts to the Lake Superior shoreline. The main trail descends from the peninsula to what appears to be a dry river channel, and here you carefully climb over layers of slate with tumbling whitewater just over your shoulder. You are only 10 minutes into the trek and already you are overwhelmed by the scenery.

On the east bank of the river, the trail ascends steeply out of the gorge to a posted junction at the top. To the south is the West River Trail, part of a 2-mile loop along the Presque Isle (see page 128). Lake Superior Trail continues east, descends in and then out of two ravines, the second time to cross Cardinal Creek a mile from the trailhead. You are never very far from the Great Lake and there is an occasional glimpse of the water, but the trail stays away from the shoreline until you reach Little Carp River.

At 2 miles you arrive at a directional sign, cross Speaker Creek and then come to the spur to **Speakers Cabin**, a four-bunk unit on the edge of a bluff overlooking Lake Superior. Speakers is only a mile from South Boundary Road via Speakers Trail, a considerably easier walk than from Presque Isle. Nearby are two **backcountry campsites**.

The Lake Superior Trail departs the spur, crosses Tiebel Creek, and then merges into an old forest road. At one point you even cross an narrow vehicle bridge built when there were eight summer cabins along the lakeshore here. Once on the other side, the trail quickly arrives at the posted junction with Speakers Trail. South Boundary Road is a 0.5 mile south from here, Presque Isle River 2.5 miles to the west, and Little Carp River 3.5 miles east.

The main trail continues to stay away from the lakeshore in a

Backpackers cross a dry channel of the Presque Isle River near the west end of the Lake Superior Trail.

thick forest for the next 3 miles but remains a somewhat level hike, if that is actually possible in this park. You cross three branches of Sahwa Creek and then Kenabeek Creek 1.5 miles from Speakers Trail. These are not the deep gorges as Cardinal Creek was nor is it difficult to keep your boots dry...unless a rain storm passes through, then you might have to search for a better ford than what the trail offers.

Not so with Pinkerton Creek, reached 5.5 miles from the Presque Isle trailhead or 3 miles from Speakers Trail. Just before reaching the west edge of gorge, the trail swings close to Lake Superior and it is easy to cut across at this point to view the water. Then you ascend slightly to the high point of 707 feet to begin a sharp descent of 60 feet to the creek, only to climb out again on the other side.

Beyond Pinkerton, the trail crosses another small creek traverse the top of a low ridge and finally comes into view of Little Carp River. Here you find yourself standing on the edge of another steep gorge. What impresses most hikers, however, is not the picturesque river and rocky ravine, but the extensive stairway and bridge across them. Just before descending, a trail leads north along the west bank and then makes a steep climb to **Little Carp Cabin**. The four-bunk cabin sits on a hill with a partial view of the river but none of the lake.

An even better setting for the night is on the east bank where the trail swings past **Little Carp River campsites**, four numbered tent pads situated in a wooded area with a view of both the river and Lake Superior. There are also a few benches built by other parties and a group fire pit.

The Little Carp River is a major crossing in the park's trail system with a posted junction on each side. On the west bank near the cabin spur is Pinkerton Trail, which reaches South Boundary Road in 3 miles. On the east side is Little Carp River Trail, which first departs south then swings east reaching Greenstone Falls in 6.5 miles, Lily Pond in 9 miles, and finally Mirror Lake in 11 miles.

On the final mile to Big Carp River the Lake Superior Trail

Lake Superior Trail near Speakers Cabin.

stays exceptionally close to the lakeshore. So close that on a windy day the surf will be crashing only a few yards away. In less than a half mile you cross a bridge over Toledo Creek, so named to remind us what little Michigan gave up to get the Porkies and the rest the Upper Peninsula. All hikers from Ohio are permitted to sit down at this point and moan.

The trail continues for another half mile before finally passing the stairway to **Big Carp River campsites**, located up on a bluff. Not far away are three cabins and the mouth of the Big Carp River, one of the most scenic areas in the park. If you are not stopping here for the evening, at least plan for a extended meal break.

The bridge over Little Carp River near Lake Superior.

7 THE LONG TRAILS

Little Carp River • Big Carp River • Government Peak

Along with the Lake Superior Trail, there are several long routes within the Porcupine Mountains that require a day or more to hike. Little Carp River extends from the Great Lake to Mirror Lake, a 11-mile trek. Big Carp River Trail is a 9-mile walk from the Escarpment to the mouth of its namesake river, and Government Peak Trail is a 7.5-mile journey from M-107, over the second highest point in the park to near Mirror Lake.

Big Carp River Trail rivals the Escarpment for panoramic overlooks and provides hikers with an excellent cross-section view of this amazing state park. Little Carp River Trail is also a scenic journey which for the most part follows the small river to its source. Both are often combined with a portion of the Lake Superior Trail to form a two- to four-day adventure.

The natural features along the Government Peak Trail are less outstanding than what is seen on the other two trails and subsequently the route receives far less foot traffic during the summer. Portions of this trail, especially around Trap Falls, make for delightful hiking and, when combined with North Mirror Lake and Escarpment, Government Peak becomes part of an excellent two to three-day outing.

🚶 LITTLE CARP RIVER TRAIL

Lake Superior To Mirror Lake
Distances: *5.5 miles to Cross Trail*
8.5 miles to Lily Pond
11 miles to Mirror Lake
Highest Point: *1,560 feet*
Hiking Time: *7 to 9 hours*
Little Carp River Trail is the second longest route in the park

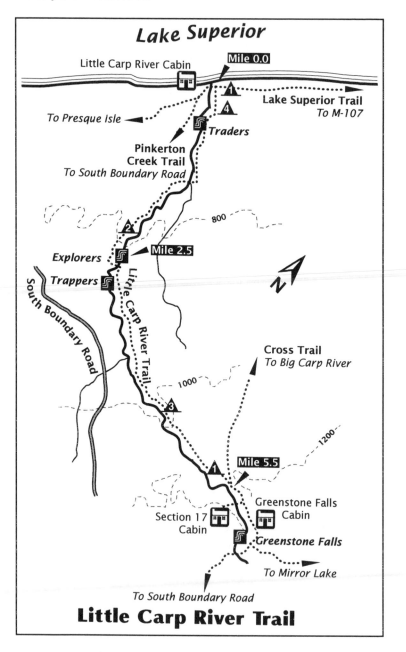

Lake Superior

Little Carp River Cabin

Mile 0.0

To Presque Isle

Lake Superior Trail
To M-107

Traders

**Pinkerton
Creek Trail**
To South Boundary Road

800

Explorers

Mile 2.5

Trappers

Little Carp River Trail

South Boundary Road

1000

Cross Trail
To Big Carp River

1200

Mile 5.5

Greenstone Falls
Cabin

Section 17
Cabin

Greenstone Falls

To Mirror Lake

To South Boundary Road

Little Carp River Trail

and one of the most scenic. You can begin near the shores of Lake Superior, elevation 611 feet, and for the most part make a gradual climb to Mirror Lake, which at 1,532 feet is the one of the highest inland lakes in the state. Along the way you pass several waterfalls, three cabins and a serene little lake in Lily Pond. The trail also connects two sets of backcountry campsites near the mouth of the Little Carp River and on Mirror Lake and passes 10 more along the way.

The western half of the trail is free of any steep climbs and now fords the river only twice having been rerouted in recent years. These bridgeless crossings are usually easy, but immediately after a heavy rainfall you might have to search for a better spot than around the trail and sometimes you might not be able to ford at all. In June of 1983 a storm dumped 13 inches of rain on the Porkies resulting in all the park's rivers becoming dangerously swollen. The worst flooding, however, occurred along the Little Carp River below Lily Pond. The water rose to depths of 30 feet, stranding several backpacking parties, wiping out bridges, and causing mudslides on bluffs and hills bordering the Little Carp.

Lake Superior To Cross Trail
Distance: 5.5 miles

Little Carp departs a junction with the Lake Superior Trail on the east side of the river and skirts the edge of the gorge briefly before descending its steep side. You can view Traders Falls on descent or cut back to the small cascade once you bottom out. From here the trail remains level for a spell, only occasionally climbing into the surrounding bluffs.

This is an extremely scenic portion of the route as you follow the flowing river through stately stands of virgin hemlock and maples. There are amble blazes and other trail signs and the path is easy to follow. Within 1.5 miles, however, you make your first ford of the day. The ford is well marked, and it is easy to identify the main route on the other side of the river. Keep in mind that there are trails along both shores of much of the river due primarily

A backpacker pauses along the Little Carp River on the way to Section 17 Cabin.

to anglers searching pools for brook trout.

The trail passes a pair of **backcountry campsites** and then arrives at Explorers Falls, 2.5 miles from Lake Superior Trail . Just beyond the falls, the trail crosses to the other side of the river, and shortly you arrive at Trappers Falls, a distinctive cascade with the water falling over a wide rock chute.

On the east side the trail has been rerouted and now for the most part follows the top of the bluffs. Along the way you pass three **backcountry campsites** that are extremely popular places to set up camp during the summer. Eventually the Little Carp Trail swings to an east-west direction, putting you on the north side, and reaches the junction with the Cross Trail, 5.5 miles from Lake Superior.

Near the junction is another **backcountry campsite** and a quarter mile beyond it you pass a stairway that leads to a foot bridge across the Little Carp River and **Section 17 Cabin** on the south side. Originally built as a ranger patrol cabin, the four-bunk unit is well secluded from trail traffic and is located on a low bluff overlooking the Little Carp River.

Cross Trail To Mirror Lake

Distance: 5.5 miles

The next leg of the trail is the hike to Lily Pond, a good 3-mile trek. A short distance from the Section 17 bridge brings you to the **Greenstone Falls Cabin**. Recently renovated, the four-bunk unit is within view of the river but not the falls themselves and is located right on the trail. The cascade is posted another 100 yards up the trail. Here the river has formed a veil of water the tumbles 15 feet down a rock embankment in a small gorge, making it a pretty little spot.

Just beyond Greenstone Falls the trail crosses a bridge over a feeder creek and then arrives at a junction with the access route from Little Carp River Road. A car parking area is only half mile away at this point with South Boundary Road 1.5 miles.

Little Carp River Trail heads east and immediately begins the steepest climb of the route. It is a steady ascent of 160 feet until you top off at the second junction to South Boundary Road. Here an old forest road passes through. Head south on it and South Boundary Road is reached in a mile. The trail continues east and in the next 0.5 mile makes a more gentle climb to 1,560 feet, the high point along the route.

You follow the ridge briefly until trail descends to cross the

Little Carp River Trail

Mile 11 · N. Mirror Lake Trail · Mirror Lake Cabins
Correction Line Trail · *To Big Carp River*
1600
4
Mirror Lake
South Mirror Lake Trail · *To Summit Peak Road*
Mile 8.5
2
Lily Pond Cabin
Beaver Creek Trail · *To Summit Peak*
2
Lily Pond
Cross Trail · *To Lake Superior*
Mile 5.5
Little Carp River Tr.
Lily Pond Trail · *To Summit Peak Rd*
1500
1600
1700
Little Carp River
To Lake Superior
1400
N
*So*uth Boundary Road

Little Carp River. Nearby are a pair of **backcountry campsites**. The Little Carp harbors populations of wild brook trout but is heavily fished in its lower sections. Anglers looking for a little adventure should search the upper portions of the river, accessing it from this crossing.

The trail makes a final climb back to 1,560 feet then descends to a posted junction with Lily Pond Trail. To the south is Lily Pond Trail; which leads 2.5 miles to Summit Peak Road. To the north is Little Carp River Trail that leads through an impressive stand of

Fording Little Carp River during an October trek.

white pine and in a half mile reaches **Lily Pond Cabin**, a four-bunk unit surrounded by the towering pines and overlooking the west end of the small lake.

The final leg of the route is the remaining 2.5 miles to Mirror Lake. The trail begins by crossing the Little Carp River where it flows out of the lake. The area is so scenic that the bridge has a bench in the middle of it. The next mile heads northeast along a fairly level route. At times in early spring and late fall, before the leaves obscure the view, you can view the ridge to southeast and spot several distinctive peaks, including Summit Peak at 1,958 feet.

Within a mile you pass the posted junction to Beaver Creek

Trail, which heads south and in a mile reaches Summit Peak parking area. Little Carp Trail swings more to the north and in the final 1.5 miles skirts its namesake river. The trail then rounds the base of a 1,600-foot high rocky knob that hikers can scramble up for a view of the Mirror Lake area. If you choose not to, the lake will come into view just before you reach the posted junction with South Mirror Lake Trail which heads south to reach Summit Peak Road in 2.5 miles. Also follow this trail to cross the Little Carp River again and pass the spur to the *Mirror Lake campsites* situated on a small inlet at the west end.

Continue heading east along the lake to pass near the *Mirror Lake Two-Bunk Cabin*, the junction to the Correction Line Trail and finally *Four-Bunk* and *Eight Bunk Cabin*. Mirror Lake marks the end of the Little Carp River Trail and is a favorite place for many backcountry users to spend an evening. The lake is set among a series of ridges and knobs, like a jewel in the mountains, with towering hemlocks and maples enclosing its shoreline. This place is stunning in late September and very much worthy of its name on any calm day.

Big Carp River Trail

Escarpment to Lake Superior
Distances: *5 miles to Correction Line Trail*
9 miles to Lake Superior
Highest Point: *1,447 feet*
Hiking Time: *5 to 7 hours*

Truly one of the most incredible hikes in the Porkies, and for that matter anywhere in Michigan, is Big River Carp Trail, a 9-mile route that begins at the Lake of the Clouds Overlook and winds it way down to shores of Lake Superior. The variety of scenery this trail passes through is amazing. Along the way there are outstanding alpine-like vistas, stands of virgin hemlock and a sheer-sided rock gorge filled by Shining Cloud Falls, one of the most spectacular cascades in the Porkies.

Big Carp River & Correction Trail

2 Backcountry Campsites

Mile 0.0

107

Mile 2   1400   Big Carp River

Miscowawbic Peak 1447 feet

Scott Creek

1200   Big Carp River Trail

LaFayette Peak 1330 feet

1200
1400
1600

1
N. Mirror Lake Trail

Mile 5

Mirror Lake Cabins

Government Peak Trail
3 To Trap Falls

Correction   Line Trail

To Lake Superior

4   Mirror Lake

Little Carp River Trail
To Lily Pond

N

The first 2 miles follow the Escarpment with only moderate climbing involved. From there the trail drops off the famous bluff and winds its way into one of the most remote corners of the park. Halfway along the route you'll pass an Adirondack shelter and at the trail's end there are three cabins near the mouth of the Carp River and backcountry campsites. Opportunities to set up camp within the gurgle of this wild river are almost unlimited.

Escarpment To Correction Line Trail
Distance: 5 miles

From the Lake of the Clouds parking lot at the end of M-107 is the posted trailhead for the route that begins at 1,246 feet. You head west into the woods only to emerge at the first of many scenic views. Within a quarter mile, the trees open up to Lake of the Clouds to the east and Big Carp River valley to the west. The trail then dips back into the wood and begins a steady ascent of 100 feet.

You top out at more than 1,400 feet to break out to a glorious view at the edge of the Escarpment. Here, Lake of the Clouds is a body of water in the distance while the valley heads west and on the horizon you can make out ridges and distinct peaks that lie outside the park. In the next mile, the trail follows the edge of this bluff, passing one spectacular view after another until arriving at a semi-open area. At 1.5 miles into the trek, you can stand on the edge of a rock cliff and peer down a sheer drop to the Big Carp River in the valley below, a stunning sight. Or you can gaze west along ridge where beyond a gap in the cliff is Miscowawbic Peak in the foreground and 2 miles away LaFayette Peak, marking one end of the Escarpment. There are a pair of **backcountry campsites** near by and it's easy to understand why they were placed here. This is a beautiful spot to set up a tent.

You resume following the bluff briefly then begin the long descent to the floor of the valley. It's a half mile descent, sharp at first but gentle most of the way as you drop from the high point of the day of 1,447 feet to less than 1,100 feet. Along the way you move from a beech/maple forest to a stand of stately hemlock.

Once in the valley, the trail continues southwest through the forest along the base of the Escarpment but remains fairly level and surprisingly dry, not the mud bath North Mirror Lake Trail can become. Even on the hottest day, it is cool and dark in the stand of hemlock where the fallen trunks, many of them victims of the 1953 tornado, are carpeted with bright green moss. At 3.5 miles you appear on the edge of a low rise, skirt it briefly then make a quick descent from hemlock into a forest of beech and maple.

The walk down the valley remains level for a mile at which point the trail passes an unofficial campsite and breaks out at the Big Carp River for the first time. Along a bridge, you cross a 15 to 20-yard wide river with a gentle flowing current that swirls through an occasional pool. Anglers would do well to drop their

A backpacker enjoys the view from the Escarpment along the Big Carp River Trail less than 2 miles from the Lake of the Clouds Overlook.

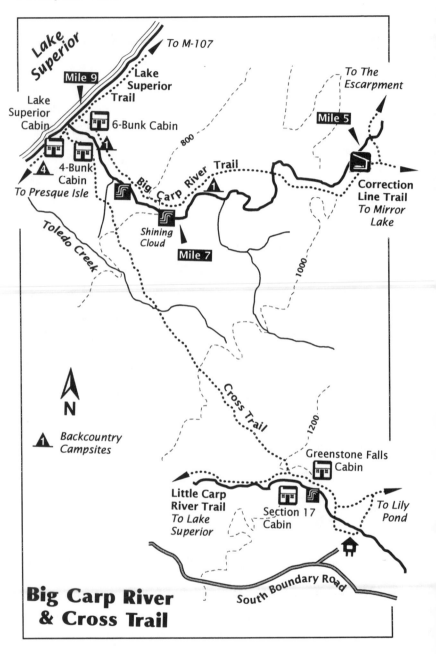

Lake Superior

To M-107

Mile 9

Lake Superior Trail

Lake Superior Cabin

6-Bunk Cabin

4-Bunk Cabin

To Presque Isle

Big Carp River Trail

800

Shining Cloud

Mile 7

To The Escarpment

Mile 5

Correction Line Trail
To Mirror Lake

1000

Toledo Creek

↑ N

⛺ *Backcountry Campsites*

Cross Trail

1200

Greenstone Falls Cabin

Little Carp River Trail
To Lake Superior

Section 17 Cabin

To Lily Pond

South Boundary Road

Big Carp River & Cross Trail

Big Carp River 6-Bunk Cabin near the mouth of the river.

packs and scout the Big Carp up stream for brook trout.

From the bridge you quickly emerge at the **Adirondack shelter**, a pleasant place to unroll a sleeping bag as the hut overlooks the river from a bluff. Some backpacker, suffering from a long night on the wooden bunk inside, inscribed on the door "Porcupine Hilton" and underneath "World Famous Firm Beds." The junction with Correction Line Trail is near by and well posted. From here Mirror Lake is a 3 miles south and 600 foot climb along the Correction Line Trail. Lake Superior is 4 miles to the north on the Big Carp River Trail.

Correction Line Trail To Lake Superior
Distance: 4 miles

Continuing toward the lakeshore, Big Carp River Trail dips into a lowlying area, crosses a wet area, and then ascends the bluffs above the river. On the high ground, you follow the river for the next mile as the trail weaves through pines and hemlocks and swings past views of the water. It is another scenic stretch of Big

Carp River Trail but it ends when you descend to ford the river. Normally the crossing is easy but this is one spot where heavy rains or April's runoff can make it a challenge to cross.

On the other side, the trail immediately makes a steep ascent up the shoreline bluff and then leaves the river as the Big Carp swings towards Lake Superior. This stretch, muddy at times but level, makes an easy stroll through another impressive stand of hemlock. Within 2 miles from the junction with the Correction Line Trail, you return to the Big Carp at the edge of a steep gorge and follow it until you are staring upriver at Shining Cloud Falls.

Many feel the falls are the most spectacular in the park. Actually Shining Cloud is a pair of cascades that make a 30 to 35-foot drop and are enclosed on one side by stone walls. You can hike down to the thundering water but take caution as it is a very a very steep drop.

The trail descends from the gorge to skirt the river itself and then for the next 0.5 mile you pass almost a dozen cascades and a **backcountry campsite**. Some are small, but four of them have drops of more than 6 feet that end in deep pools. Downstate they would be the center piece of a state park, but here they are so common place they are unnamed and left off the park maps. Less than a mile from departing Shining Cloud you come to an area where Big Carp River levels out at a spot posted "Bathtub Falls." The falls are really a series of one-foot drops and pools. It's so close to the end of a long day, however, that more than one backpacker has soaked his weary feet in this natural ice-cold jacuzzi.

Originally the trail at this point crossed the river and merged into the Cross Trail. A few trail signs still mark the way, but now the route leads you away from the river and makes a steep climb, via a series of switchbacks up a river bluff. You top off to one more panorama where far below is the Big Carp River flowing past you and on the horizon you can view Lake Superior for the first time.

For the remaining half mile you hug the edge of the bluff and then descend to **Big Carp River Six-Bunk Cabin** near the mouth of the river. This is one of the most scenic spots in the park and

The Adirondack shelter on the Big Carp River Trail.

a popular place to spend the night. Across the bridge, is the posted end of the Cross Trail and the **Big Carp River Four Bunk Cabin**. Follow Lake Superior Trail west a short way and you will pass **Lake Superior Cabin**, a four-bunk unit then come to the stairs that lead to the **Big Carp River campsites**.

GOVERNMENT PEAK TRAIL

M-107 to North Mirror Lake Trail

Distances: *2 miles to Union Springs Trail*

2.6 miles to trailside shelter

3 miles to Lost Lake Trail

7.5 miles to North Mirror Lake Trail

Highest Point: *1,850 feet*

Hiking Time: *5 to 7 hours*

This is a 7.5-mile route that extends from a trailhead off M-107, heads south to a junction with Lost Lake Trail and then west to merge into North Mirror Lake Trail, a mile from the popular lake. The first half, especially the area around Trap Falls, is very scenic and features both backcountry campsites and an Adirondack shelter.

The second half is a lightly traveled route where at times the brush is so thick during the summer that it obscures the path. This portion of the trail is not nearly as interesting, and while Government Peak may be the second highest point of the Porkies, the view at best is a very limited one from the top.

The trail, however, can be combined with North Mirror and the Escarpment trails to form a 16-mile loop with nights spent near Trap Falls and Mirror Lake. If you are contemplating this scenic trek, begin with Government Peak and follow North Mirror Lake Trail downhill to Lake of the Clouds, by far the easiest way to hike this trail.

M-107 To Lost Lake Trail
Distance: 3 miles

Government Peak Trail begins along M-107, 4 miles from the Escarpment Overlook. You begin with a steep climb to quickly pass the posted east end of the Escarpment Trail and then the first trailhead to the Overlook Trail. The trail levels out and then descends to the second trailhead of the Overlook, a 3-mile loop that climbs to 1,500 feet. Here you find a huge trail sign that declares you have just hiked a mile from M-107. It is the fastest mile most backpackers have ever covered.

Government Peak continues south and crosses through a low-lying forest, a level but often wet and muddy stretch. Within a true mile from M-107 you cross Upper Carp River for the first time, a sluggish stream in a marshy area. But all this changes in a half mile. The trail cuts across the wide bend where the river swings west, and when it returns to the Upper Carp you are climbing through an old growth forest with a mountain stream gurgling along side of you.

This is very scenic gorge-like area is reached 1.5 miles from M-107 and located nearby are a pair of **backcountry campsites** with

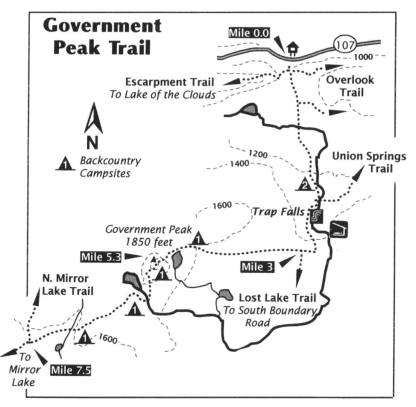

Government Peak Trail

Mile 0.0

107

1000

Escarpment Trail
To Lake of the Clouds

Overlook Trail

N

Backcountry Campsites

1200
1400

Union Springs Trail

1600

Trap Falls

Government Peak 1850 feet

Mile 5.3

N. Mirror Lake Trail

Mile 3

Lost Lake Trail
To South Boundary Road

1600

To Mirror Lake

Mile 7.5

fire rings and view of the river. You continue to climb into the gorge for the next half mile along a river that churns and swirls through an obstacle course of boulders, rocks, and ancient trees that have fallen across the water. The posted junction with Union Spring Trail is reached 2 miles from the start. By heading east on this trail you can reach the natural spring in 2 miles and South Boundary Road in 4 miles.

Government Peak continues climbing south and passes several scenic pools with the best one , Trap Falls, reached 0.4 mile from the junction. The cascade is well named as the Upper Carp tumbles 15 feet down a narrow rock ledge into a basin below that traps the river momentarily into a deep pool before letting it continue. A bench in a stand of towering pines completes this scenic spot but

A backpacker heads towards the Escarpment from Mirror Lake.

on a hot summer day you will find that many backpackers would rather sit in the pool than on the bench.

Less than a quarter mile up the trail the **Adirondack shelter** is reached. It is reached with an easy ford to the other side of the Upper Carp and is situated near the river but not on it. Government Peak continues by climbing a small hill and then descends to the Junction with Lost Lake Trail, 3 miles from M-107. Lost Lake Trail leads to its namesake lake in 2.5 miles and South Boundary Road in 4.5 miles.

Lost Lake To North Mirror Lake
Distance: 4.5 miles

At this point Government Peak swings west and begins its second half as a fairly level route. Within a mile the trail climbs a series of low ridges and crosses several small streams that are often dry during mid-summer. After the third stream, the trail levels out and 1.8 miles from the Lost Lake junction you break out at an open marsh with a large beaver pond in the middle. The pond is the headwaters for the Upper Carp and good place to sight a variety of wildlife including beavers, deer and waterfowl. There is a ***backcountry campsite*** nearby

Once you skirt the pond, the trail begins its ascent to Government Peak. It is a steady climb up and steep at times, but in less than a half mile you reach the peak where its elevation of 1,850 feet is posted near the stone foundations of a 1927 fire tower. The peak is reached 5.3 miles from M-107 and for most backpackers the view is anticlimactic. On the west side, however, it is possible to gaze through the trees into the interior of the park. There is a ***backcountry campsite*** near the peak and another on its west side.

Descending the peak to the west is at first a rapid downhill hike but overall not the steep slope experienced on the east side. Within a half mile you bottom out at a small creek and from there the trail is a level woods walk for the remaining 2 miles. This is where the trail can really be obscure and sometimes very muddy but eventually you reach the junction with North Mirror Lake Trail. The west end of Government Peak Trail is an easy mile from Mirror Lake and 3 miles from the Lake of the Clouds Overlook.

Dayhiker crossing a marsh on the Beaver Creek Trail.

8 The Short Trails

Lost Lake • Correction Line • South and North Mirror Lake • Pinkerton • Cross Trail

Within the backcountry are a number of shorter trails that either serve as links between longer routes or provide access into the park from a road.

Correction Line Trail links Big Carp River with the trails at Mirror Lake while Cross Trail spans from Lake Superior Trail at the mouth of the Big Carp to Greenstone Falls. Pinkerton, Lost Lake and the Mirror Lake trails all provide access from South Boundary Road or, in the case of North Mirror Lake, from the Lake of the Clouds Overlook.

Dayhikers looking for possible routes should consider hiking into Lost Lake, a scenic stretch that makes for a round trip of 4 miles, or combine South Mirror Lake with a portion of Little Carp Trail, Beaver Creek Trail and Summit Trail for a 5.5-mile loop that begins and ends at the top of Summit Peak Road.

Lost Lake Trail

South Boundary Road To Government Peak Trail

Distance: *2 miles to Lost Lake*
2.7 miles to Upper Carp River
4.5 miles To Government Peak Trail

Highest Point: *1,560 feet*

Hiking Time: *3 to 4 hours one-way*

This trail extends from South Boundary Road to Government Peak Trail and along the way passes its namesake lake; a small, remote, and beautiful body of water. There is considerable climbing and a steep descent on this route but much of it is

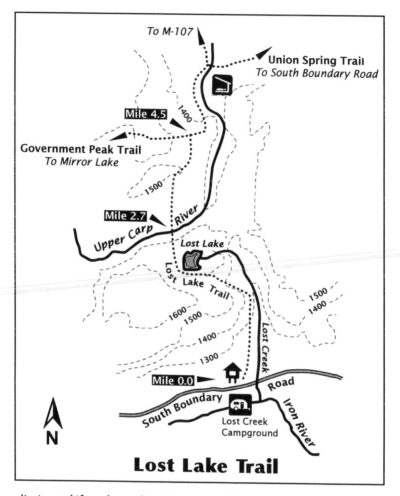

To M-107

Union Spring Trail
To South Boundary Road

Mile 4.5

1400

Government Peak Trail
To Mirror Lake

1500

Mile 2.7

Upper Carp River

Lost Lake

Lost Lake Trail

1500
1400

1600
1500

1400

1300

Mile 0.0

Lost Creek Road

South Boundary

Iron River

Lost Creek
Campground

N

Lost Lake Trail

eliminated if you're only going to the lake itself, a moderately easy round-trip hike of 4 miles.

The trailhead is posted along South Boundary Road, 7 miles from M-107 and across from Lost Creek Outpost Campground where there is a hiker's parking area. The route begins as a level path through pines and hardwoods and within a half mile appears like the old mining road that it is. The trail\road is carved into the side of a narrow ravine and a gentle climb soon puts you above Lost

Creek with a scenic view of the water rushing below.

Within a mile, the trail crosses a feeder creek. A few yards away there is a picturesque pool and a small cascade spilling into Lost Creek. At this point the trail departs the mining road and begins a steep ascent to the higher level of the lake. You climb for almost a mile until you top off at 1,560 feet in a virgin stand of hemlock and then emerge from the giant trees for your first view of the lake.

The small lake is really more like a very large pond with a shoreline guarded by a tangle of brush, an angler's nightmare if trying to cast from the edge. A belly boat would be excellent here though the lake is not stocked and few people brother to fish it. Waterfowl often gather at Lost Lake, and occasionally you can spot a deer feeding along the edge.

The trail skirts the south side of the lake, arriving at a mileage sign at its southwest corner that informs you Government Peak Trail is still 2.5 miles away. From here the pines give way to a hardwood forest with thick underbrush, and the trail crosses the often wet west end of Lost Lake to begin a rapid descent. In the next half mile, you are gripping the straps of your backpack as the trail descends almost 160 feet off the ridge.

At 2.7 miles you bottom out at Upper Carp River. The headwaters for this river are ponds near Government Peak. From there the Upper Carp makes a loop to the south then north before eventually emptying into Lake of the Clouds. This is one of most scenic stretches of the river as well as one of most remote. Anglers willing to bash some heavy brush might be rewarded with some excellent brook trout fishing by exploring downstream segments.

There is no bridge across Upper Carp and although the river is considerably larger than Lost Creek, it is an easy ford during normal water levels. On the other side the trail climbs out of the Upper Carp valley in the final mile but it is not nearly as steep as the south side. You gain only 80 feet before arriving at Government Peak Trail at a posted junction.

For those continuing on, Government Peak, the second

highest point in the park, is 1.3 miles to the west and Mirror Lake lies 4.5 miles along Government Peak Trail. An Adirondack shelter is less than a half mile north along the same trail and M-107 is 3 miles. To the west along Government Peak Trail are four **backcountry campsites**.

CORRECTION LINE TRAIL

Big Carp River To Mirror Lake
Map on page 85
Distance: *3 miles*
Highest Point: *1,600 feet*
Hiking Time: *1.5 to 2 hours*

Correction Line Trail is a well traveled route that connects Big Carp River Trail, 4 miles from Lake Superior or 5 miles from the Lake of the clouds Overlook, to Mirror Lake. It's commonly used to form a loop from Lake Superior to Mirror Lake and back to M-107. By combining portions of Lake Superior Trail and Big Carp River and returning on Correction Line and North Mirror Lake Trail, backpackers can undertake a 20-mile, three to four-day trip through some of the most scenic sections of the Porkies.

Named for the "correction line" cartographers use to adjust flat maps to the earth's curvature, the trail departs Big Carp River from a junction near the **Adirondack shelter**. The first part lies in a low-lying forest that is notorious for being muddy even in fair weather. After a heavy rain, the mud can suck your boots off.

Within 0.7 mile you cross Landlookers Creek. Landlookers were timber cruisers hired by the lumber companies in the 19th century to search and map out stands of pine. Ironically, this is one section the lumber barons never touched as much of Correction Line passes through virgin stands of hemlock as well as impressive tracts of maples and yellow birch. Once across the creek, the trail begins it long climb to the higher level of the lake.

You climb 200 feet in the next half mile where the trail crosses a small creek and crosses to the other side of a ravine. Then you

An eight-point buck stands on the edge of a meadow.

begin climbing again, this time along a much steeper section as Correction Line takes you quickly from 1,300 to 1,584 feet. You top off on the edge of Big Carp River drainage and, in the fall, views of the valley below are possible.

The trail levels out when it enters a small hollow of old growth timber enclosed to the north by impressive rock bluffs. The only thing more impressive is the mud. It gets deeper still. The natural inclination is to hike around the mud holes but that only makes the

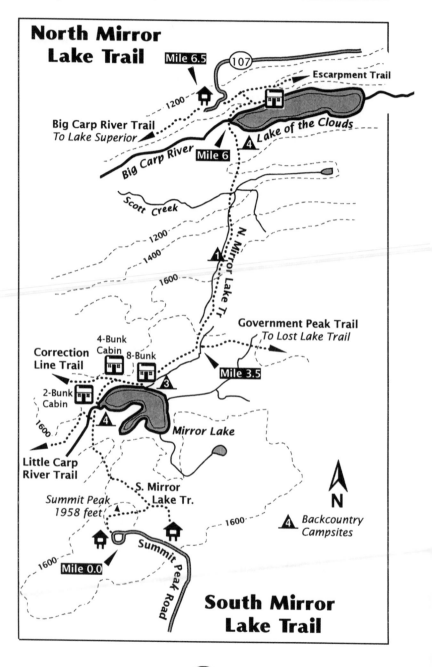

North Mirror Lake Trail

Mile 6.5

107

Escarpment Trail

1200

Lake of the Clouds

Big Carp River Trail
To Lake Superior

Big Carp River Mile 6

4

Scott Creek

1200

1400

1600

1

N. Mirror Lake Tr.

Government Peak Trail
To Lost Lake Trail

4-Bunk Cabin

Correction Line Trail

8-Bunk

Mile 3.5

2-Bunk Cabin

3

1600

4

Mirror Lake

Little Carp River Trail

S. Mirror Lake Tr.

Summit Peak 1958 feet

1600

N

4 *Backcountry Campsites*

Mile 0.0

Summit Peak Road

1600

South Mirror Lake Trail

situation worse for others. It is really best to hike right through the mud and wash your boots at the end of the day.

The final half mile begins with a climb over a 1,600-foot knob and ends with the lake coming into view for the first time. A rapid descent puts you at Mirror Lake's north shoreline and a posted junction where the trail ends. Lake Superior is 11 miles to the west via the Little Carp River Trail and departing east here is North Mirror Lake Trail, which reaches the Lake of the Clouds Overlook in 4 miles. Follow Little Carp River Trail to pass the **Two-Bunk Cabin** and then the South Mirror Lake Trail to reach four **backcountry campsites**. Head east to check out the other cabins and other campsites.

South & North Mirror Lake Trails
South Boundary Road To Escarpment Overlook
Distance: *2.5 miles to Mirror Lake (via South Trail)*
6.5 miles To Escarpment Overlook
Highest Point: *1,760 feet*
Hiking Time: *4 to 5 hours*

The North and South Mirror Lake Trails provide a route that crosses the heart of the Porkies, beginning from Summit Peak Road and ending at the Lake of the Clouds Overlook. The highest point is quickly reached along the southern portion, but the northern half features the most climbing, especially if you are hiking into the lake from the Escarpment.

The South Trail is the shortest and easiest route to popular Mirror Lake with its three cabins and backcountry campsites, a trek of only 2.5 miles. North Mirror Lake Trail is often used as a return to the M-107 for backpackers who begin on the Lake Superior Trail. For that reason, it will be described from south to north, by far the easiest way to hike this rugged route.

South Mirror Trail
Distance: 2.5 Miles To Mirror Lake
A trailhead with limited parking is located 1.5 miles up Summit

Peak Road. If the parking area is full, a larger one for overflow is located at the beginning of the road. The trail departs north from here as a forest road that is used off-season by the staff as a service drive into the heart of the park.

You climb more than 200 feet from your car or the trailhead, topping off at 1,760 feet in the first half mile. At this point the trail begins to skirt Summit Peak. At 1,958 feet, Summit Peak is the highest point in the park and third highest in the state. Eventually the trail descends the ridge and quickly arrives at a posted junction with the Summit Peak Trail, 1.2 miles from the trailhead. The view from the peak is nice, but it is a steep, 258-foot climb to the top from here.

South Mirror Lake Trail continues north as a forest road descending gently until it bottoms out at small stream and becomes a true foot path 1.8 miles into the hike. On the other side it climbs to 1,640 feet, crosses a ridge and then descends to the Little Carp River. Just before crossing the river, you pass the spur that leads to four **backcountry campsites** located on a long inlet that forms the west end of the lake.

On the other side is the posted junction with Little Carp River Trail. From here Lily Pond is 2.5 miles to the west and the three cabins on the north side a short walk to the east. At 1,532 feet, Mirror Lake is the highest lake in the park and one of the highest in the state. It is surrounded by rugged bluffs and ridges, many which can be climbed for views of the area, while towering pines dominate much of the shoreline. The trail skirts the lake first passing a spur to the **Two-Bunk Cabin** and later a posted junction to Correction Line Trail.

Just beyond the junction is the **Four-Bunk Cabin** located near the lake in a stand of towering pine. Finally you reach the **Eight-Bunk Cabin**, a virtual log lodge perched right above the water. You need to continued along the trail past the large cabin to pick up the North Mirror Lake Trail or reach three more **backcountry campsites** along the east side of the lake.

The bridge and broadwalk at the west end of Lake of the Clouds.

The view at the end of North Mirror Lake Trail.

North Mirror Lake Trail

Distances: 1 mile to Government Peak Trail
3.5 miles to Lake of the Clouds
4 miles To Escarpment

North Mirror Lake Trail extends from the lake to the Lake of the Clouds Overlook, a 4-mile trek that takes most hikers almost good three hours to walk. From the shoreline, the North Mirror Lake quickly crosses a creek and then parallels Trail Creek as it climbs a low ridge. This section is often wet and muddy from heavy use even though you are well above the creek. Within a mile you come to the posted junction with the Government Peak Trail.

Government Peak heads east to reach the 1850-foot high point in 2 miles. North Mirror Lake Trail departs the junction to the north and begins a gentle ascent while in a mile you top off at 1640 feet. This stretch can also be muddy at times but scenic in

October when the fallen leaves give way to views of 1700-foot ridges on both sides of you. Nearby is a **backcountry campsite**.

Beyond the ridges, the trail begins a long descent, easy walking at first, but 2 miles from the lake the trek becomes a knee-bending drop. If coming from the Lake of the Clouds Overlook, you will find this is one of the steepest climbs in the park. In 0.75 mile, you descend from 1,640 feet to 1,160 through a gorge-like area where a tributary of Scott Creek rushes downhill. Keep your eyes peeled for trail blazes in the trees as it's easy to get turned around here.

You bottom out to cross Scott Creek, climb over a 1,200-foot ridge and at 3.5 miles from the lake arrive at the west end of Lake of the Clouds. A spur heads left to a series of four **backcountry campsites**. A long boardwalk crosses a stream emptying into the lake here and makes for a unique viewing point. You can not see much of the famous lake but you can look above to spot people staring down at you from the Lake of the Clouds Overlook.

The trail swings to the east, skirts the shoreline of the lake and then comes to the spur that leads to the **Lake of Cloud Cabin** a quarter mile away. The final half mile is a steep march uphill as the trail becomes a series of switchbacks, gaining more than 150 feet from the level of the lake until finally breaking out at the M-107 parking lot at 1,246 feet. Along the way you pass a posted junction to west end of the Escarpment Trail.

PINKERTON TRAIL

South Boundary Road To Little Carp River Trail
Distance: *3 miles*
Highest Point: *1,060 feet*
Hiking Time: *1 to 2 hours*

Pinkerton Trail is the shortest route to the cabins and campsites near the mouth of the Big Carp River, a popular destination for many hikers. The trail itself is 3 miles, making the journey to the Big Carp a one-way trek of roughly 4 miles. Pinkerton is also a scenic walk, passing through impressive stands

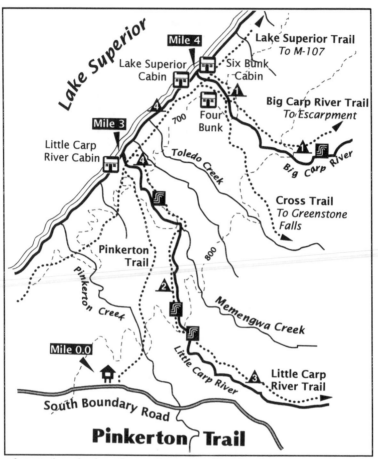

Pinkerton Trail

of virgin hemlock and crossing several bridged streams and creeks along the way.

The trailhead is posted along South Boundary Road, 5 miles east of Presque Isle and 20 miles west from the Visitor's Center. There is limited parking here.

From the trailhead you quickly enter the old growth forest, a stand of impressive hemlocks and later northern hardwoods such as maple and yellow birch. The trail begins with a mild descent through the forest and within a mile arrives at the Pinkerton Creek bridge. On the other side you climb the bank, level out briefly, then descend to cross a feeder creek on a slab bridge.

The trail levels out after this, angling towards Little Carp River through the impressive forest and at one point passes a lighting-struck tree posted with "1988", the year of the storm. Within 1.5 miles of crossing Pinkerton, you emerge on the edge of the Little Carp River Gorge to see the rushing stream below. From here it is a gradual hlaf mile descent to the Lake Superior Trail junction.

To the west Presque Isle River is a 6-mile trek while **Little Carp River Cabin** is just up the trail to the east. The mouth of the Big Carp River is still more than a mile to the east but reached along a very scenic stretch of the Lake Superior Trail that hugs the shoreline.

Cross Trail

Lake Superior To Greenstone Falls
Map on page 88
Distance: *5 miles to Little Carp River Trail*
Highest Point: *1,220 feet*
Hiking Time: *3 to 4 hours*

Cross Trail is the least traveled route in the park. It connects the Lake Superior Trail at the mouth of the Big Carp River with the Little Carp River Trail near Greenstone Falls. It is a 5-mile trek, but most backpackers choose to follow Little Carp River instead, a longer hike (6.5 miles to the Greenstone Falls) but a much more scenic route. Or if they are entering the park, they reach the Big Carp River via Pinkerton and Lake Superior trails, a 4-mile walk.

Cross Trail is level for the most part but can be wet, especially in the middle when it crosses Memengwa Swamp, and at times hard to follow. But since there are usually few people on the trail, chances of spotting wildlife are excellent. In most places there will be far more deer tracks in the mud than foot prints and it is rare to hike this trail without seeing at least one set of bear prints.

From the west bank of the Big Carp River the trail is posted at its junction with the Lake Superior Trail and immediately passes

Hiker crosses the Memengwa Swamp along Cross Trail.

the four-bunk cabin. The trail stays near the river for the next half mile, winding along a series of interesting pools until you reach Bathtub Falls. At one time this was the start of the Big Carp River Trail and a set of orange blazes still marks where you would have crossed the river.

At this point Cross Trail swings away from the water and makes its steepest climb of the day. You ascend more than 80 feet to the top of a bluff and are rewarded with a fine view of the Big Carp flowing through a series of rapids far below. You follow the river briefly, then the trail swings away from the Big Carp for good, and in a half mile you descend to cross a feeder creek.

Cross Trail then turns into a woods walk through an old growth forest for the next mile and is level with the exception of crossing three streams. The third is Toledo Creek that flows through a small ravine. You remain in the forest for another half mile and then enter the wet section of the route, 3 miles from Lake Superior.

This is sloppy hiking with mud burying your boots even during a dry spell. It will also be "buggy", but there is one plus. Wildlife tracks will be all around you. The half-pear prints of whitetail deer will be the most common tracks seen. But look around, if the deer flies will allow it, and there's a good chance you will spot bear prints. Bear tracks look more like a human foot than they do dog tracks, but they have a larger, more rounded pad and often the claws are clearly visible. Those more than four inches wide indicate a good size bruin has passed through.

Within a half mile the wet lowlying woods turns into a grassy marsh-like opening before Cross Trail returns to the woods. In all, it is roughly a mile of hard slogging before you leave the swamp behind and enter the final portion of the trail, a very gradual ascent through a pleasant stand hemlock to the high point of 1,220 feet. From here you drop quickly to the Little Carp Trail junction.

At this point **Section 17 Cabin** lies just across the river. **Greenstone Falls Cabin** is a quarter mile west along Little Carp River Trail and Mirror Lake is a little more than 6 miles.

The lookout tower at Summit Peak, the highest point in the Porkies and the third highest in Michigan at 1,958 feet.

9 Dayhikes

Escarpment Trail • Overlook Trail • Whitetail Path • Visitor Center Nature Trail • Union Mine Trail • Union Spring Trail • Summit Peak Trail • Beaver Creek and Lily Pond Trails • Greenstone Falls Access Trail • East and West River Trails

Need to stretch your legs? Have a spare hour in the park or an afternoon? Or are some of your hiking partners too young to tackle the 16-mile-long Lake Superior Trail? Porcupine Mountains may be a wilderness but it's also a state park with a wide variety of hiking opportunities. Many trails around its perimeter make for excellent dayhikes.

The best, by far, is the 4-mile-long Escarpment Trail, perhaps the most scenic foot path in the Midwest. Others are scenic loops, including East\West River Trails, Overlook Trail, and Summit Peak Trail when combined with a portion of South Mirror Lake Trail.

If young children are a part of your hiking party, try the Union Mine Trail, the Access Trail to Greenstone Falls or the East\West River Trails. All three treks are 2 miles or shorter in length and can be handled by most children as young as four or five years old.

Perhaps the most popular short hike in the park is the descent from the Escarpment along North Mirror Lake Trail to the bridge across Big Carp River and then the steep climb back up, a round trip of 1.5 miles. The start of other long trails that make for scenic dayhikes include the

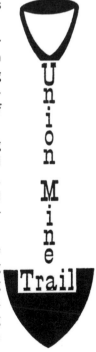

first 2 miles of Big Crap River Trail (see page 85) and the beginning of the Lake Superior Trail from M-107 (see page 66).

🏃 Escarpment Trail

Lake of the Clouds to Government Peak Trail
Distance: *4 miles*
Highest Point: *1,600 feet*
Hiking Time: *2 to 3 hours*

This is the crowning jewel of trails not only in the Porkies but in all of Michigan and possibly in the Midwest. The Escarpment combines a high rocky bluff and alpine-like vistas with views of the park's rugged interior, Big Carp River Valley and, of course, the center piece of the park; Lake of Clouds. Unlike the tourists who simply drive to the overlook and look down, the Escarpment Trail provides you with view of the famous lake from several different angles, and if the day is clear, you can easily shoot off a roll of film or more by the time you return to M-107.

The only drawback is that the Escarpment is a point-to-point trail. You begin here, you end up over there 4 miles from your vehicle. There is a spur reached halfway along the trail that can be used to access M-107 after two miles and, of course, you can always turn around and simply retrace your steps. However, it would be a shame to go that far to hike one of the most awe-inspiring trails in the Midwest and not finish it.

The easiest direction to follow the route is beginning from the Lake of the Clouds Overlook. Before departing remember to fill the water bottles. There is no drinking water at the overlook, and on a clear summer day the route across the Escarpment can be a hot one. You actually begin at the posted North Mirror Lake Trailhead and for a half mile the trail dips and climbs along the Escarpment as a rock and boulder-strewn path.

At a posted junction, North Mirror Lake Trail plummets towards Lake of the Clouds while the Escarpment officially begins with a climb through a mix forest of pines and young oaks. Quickly you arrive at the first overlook, staring down at middle of the lake.

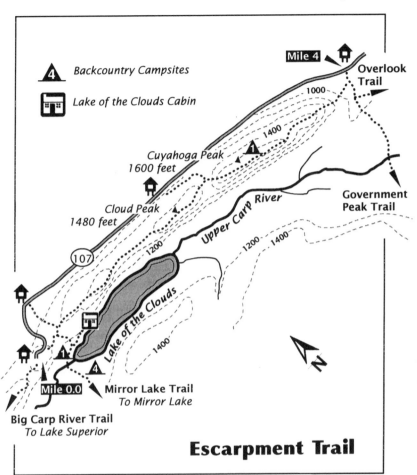

Backcountry Campsites

Lake of the Clouds Cabin

Mile 4

Overlook Trail

1000

1400

Cuyahoga Peak
1600 feet

Cloud Peak
1480 feet

Upper Carp River

Government
Peak Trail

107

1200

1200 1400

Lake of the Clouds

1400

Mile 0.0

Mirror Lake Trail
To Mirror Lake

Big Carp River Trail
To Lake Superior

Escarpment Trail

The trail resumes with a sharper climb and in half mile you break out at a second vista. This vista is spectacular, as good or better than overlook at the end of M-107 because you're at a much higher at 1,480. At your feet, 400 feet straight down, is Lake of the Clouds in royal blue. To the west you can see visitors who have just stepped out of their cars and to the east is the rest of the Escarpment and the Upper Carp River winding its way into the lake.

The trail continues along the open cliff for a few hundred yards

Escarpment Trail offers alpine-like vistas of Lake of the Clouds.

where you enjoy the scenery every step of the way before dipping into the woods. You cross two small knobs, one with a view, make a rapid descent, and then begin the climb to Cloud Peak. The trail skirts the 1,514-foot high point, and for the first time in the hike you are standing at the east end of the lake and viewing it in it's entirely to the west along with the rocky bluff. It is even possible to see a portion of Government Peak on the horizon to the south.

At one time this spectacular view was the only view for most people. Before the Porkies became a state park in 1945, M-107 ended 2 miles short of where it does today, and visitors were faced with a half mile trek to Cloud Peak to see Lake of the Clouds. From the peak, the trail makes another rapid descent to a posted junction 2 miles into the hike. A short spur departs north from here to descend quickly to M-107 and can be used to turn the first half of the Escarpment Trail into a 4-mile loop with a return along the park road.

Continuing south, the trail quickly passes the posted site of Carp Lake Mine. Carp Lake was the name for Lake of the Clouds when the mine was established in 1858. The operation lingered into the 1920s but reached its peak in 1865 when a company of more than 50 men used a small stamping mill to produce 13,000 pounds of copper from several shafts into the Escarpment. Near the trail is a fenced-off cistern where a spur leads down the slope to the twin boilers of the stamping mill that can still be seen today.

You depart the mine site by immediately ascending towards Cuyahoga Peak, climbing more than 200 feet to the highpoint of the day of 1,600 feet. In less than a half mile from the junction, you breakout to another panoramic scene of the Upper Carp River where the trail skirts the edge of the Escarpment. You have passed Cuyahoga Peak though it's difficult to know exactly when. What you do notice is a posted **backcountry campsite**. What a site! There is a fire ring and space for maybe only one or two tents, but it is situated near the edge of the bluff where campers can enjoy an alpine-like view from their sleeping bags in the morning.

The trail continues by beginning its long descent off the Escarpment. You quickly pass the only view of Lake Superior and then begin a steep portion of the descent. The trail levels out briefly to pass Cuyahoga Mine posted with the year "1856." The mine never produced a profitable amount of copper and probably died out in 1866 when Carp Lake mine was first shut down. All that remains today is a long open ditch-like digging.

The mine is only a quarter mile from the trail's east end but it is a steep quarter mile and you're practically running downhill when you arrive at the junction with Government Peak. Head north to reach M-107 in a quarter mile and south to stay in the interior of park along Government Peak Trail.

Overlook Trail
Round Trip From M-107
Distance: *3.5 miles*
Highest Point: *1,510 feet*
Hiking Time: *2 to 4 hours*

The Overlook Trail offers one of the few loops into the rugged interior of the park that is under 10 miles in length, making it an ideal dayhike for those with only a few hours left on their itinerary. The trail begins and ends off M-107, climbs to 1,500 feet and passes two viewing areas that provide a glimpse into the heart of the Porkies. All this on a hike that's only 3.5 miles long. But don't be mislead by the short distance. This is still a challenging trek with long steep climbs and poor footings in many places.

You pick up the Overlook at the Government Peak Trailhead, posted along M-107 3.5 miles west of South Boundary Road. You actually begin and end on Government Peak Trail but only briefly. The wide trail quickly climbs to its junction with the Escarpment Trail, then intersects with the north end of the Overlook, a junction that can be easily missed by those not looking for it.

The Overlook begins by descending to a small stream, climbing out of the gully, and then passing through a wet area for the next 0.3 mile. This ends when the trail enters a stand of stately virgin hemlock. The trees are stunning, especially when most people have to lean back to see the tops. At this point keep a sharp eye out for trail blazes on the trunks as the trail is not well defined in places.

A half mile into the hike the Overlook begins a steady climb, levels out briefly among the towering pines and climbs again. The second ascent is a steep one for more than a quarter mile before you top out in a forest of hardwoods at 1,510 feet. Here the foot path merges with a two-track that is a ski trail during the winter.

The first view is only a short descent away, and you reach it 1.6 miles into the hike. Referred to as the West Vista, the high point is far better in September, when leaves have fallen and the rest are changing color. In the winter, it is the highlight for many cross country skiers as they can look down the Carp River Valley, past Lake of the Clouds and the Escarpment all the way to Lake Superior.

From this overlook, the trail loses much of the elevation, you have just worked so hard to gain, in a rapid drop of 140 feet through mostly virgin pines. At 2.2 miles you come to the second viewing point of the park's interior, The view depends on the

Overlook & Union Spring Trail

season. In mid-summer, you have to stand on your toes to get a glimpse south of the park's rugged interior.

The trail continues with another sharp descent of 180 feet and at 2.4 miles levels out in a stand of pines. Keep an eye out for tree blazes here as they will lead through the pines for the next half mile to a well-posted junction with Government Peak Trail. Although the sign says it is a mile to M-107, it's actually much closer to a half mile. The trail crosses a wet area that is well planked and then climbs slightly as a wide, unmistakable path. You finish off the day with a descent to M-107, passing the earlier junctions to the Escarpment and Overlook.

🚶 Whitetail Path

Union Bay Campground to the Visitor Center
Distance: *1 mile*
Highest Point: *660 feet*
Hiking Time: *30 minutes*

Whitetail Path begins on the south side of M-107 near Union Bay Campground and parallels the state road before swinging south to emerge at the parking lot of the Visitor's Center. The trail is used primarily by campers to reach the interpretive center or park headquarters.

🚶 Visitor Center Nature Trail

Round Trip From Visitor Center
Distance: *1 mile*
Highest Point: *700 feet*
Hiking Time: *30 to 45 minutes*

Just off the entrance of the Visitor Center is the start of this nature trail, a mile-long loop with a series of interpretive plaques along it. The trail heads south, passes the park headquarters and then briefly merges into an old logging road that is also part of the cross country ski network during the winter. Eventually you come to a junction with the Whitetail Path just before arriving at the Visitor Center parking lot.

🚶 Union Mine Trail

Round Trip From South Boundary Road
Distance: *1 mile*
Highest Point: *880 feet*
Hiking Time: *30 to 45 minutes*

Union Main Trail is the other interpretive trail in the park and features 17 numbered posts that correspond to an informative brochure. The brochure is available at the Visitor's Center or during the summer at the trailhead parking lot, reached 1.7 miles south of M-107 on South Boundary Road.

The trail is posted on the north side of the parking lot and hiked in clockwise direction by first heading towards Union River. You immediately reach the site of Union Mine where post number one marks the oldest copper operation in the Porkies, dating back to 1845 when the first shaft was sunk.

At Union River, the trail descends downstream, crosses South Boundary Road and just before reaching Union River Outpost Campground cuts across to Little Union River. At either of the rivers it is possible to leave the trail and continue downstream to view a number of small cascades that form during the spring or after heavy rainfalls. The last leg of the trail is to follow Little Union River upstream back across South Boundary Road to the parking lot. The trail overall is easy but this stretch involves climbing about 100 feet.

☗ Union Spring Trail
South Boundary Rd. To Government Pk. Trail
Distance: *4 miles*
Highest Point: *1,300 feet*
Hiking Time: *2 to 3 hours*

Technically Union Spring Trail is an access route into the park's interior and not a dayhike as it extends 4 miles from South Boundary Road to Government Peak Trail. Along the way it passes the second largest natural spring in Michigan, and that's the reason most visitors walk the trail. A trek just to the spring and back makes for an enjoyable and easy 4-mile hike highlighted by the crystal clear pool of Union Spring.

The trail also passes a pair of backcountry campsites near an impoundment. These sites are an ideal designation for a family interested in an overnight trip to ease young children into backpacking. Children as young as 5 years old can easily handle the 1.5-mile level walk to the backcountry sites.

The trailhead for Union Spring is on South Boundary Road 2 miles south of M-107, just beyond the posted Union Mine Trail. The walk begins on an old logging road that quickly crosses Little Union River and in half mile comes to a locked gate. Beyond the

The view of the Porkies from Summit Peak Trail.

gate, the forest closes in as the trail crosses Union River and then makes a short ascent, the only climb on the way to the spring.

You pass the posted spur to **Union River Cabin** and within a mile from the trailhead come to a junction. The trail heads west at this point. Continuing in a northwest direction is an old logging road that is groomed in the winter for cross country skiers. From the junction the Union Spring Impoundment is quickly reached and nearby are the **backcountry campsites**, consisting of two tent pads and fire rings.

The spring itself is another half mile along a level route through old growth hardwoods and hemlock. The route can be wet at times, but the surrounding forest is impressive. Union Spring appears as small pond with a viewing platform extending out to the middle of it. From the end of the platform, you can gaze into the deep but clear pool to see the spring bubbling out of the ground at more than 700 gallons a minute.

The spring marks the halfway point to Government Peak Trail and the remaining 2 miles begin in a lowlying, marshy area. A good place to spot wildlife. A bad place to be without bug dope. Within a mile of the spring the trail curves to the south and begins a steady ascent of more than 100 feet. You actually top off at 1,300 feet and from there descend quickly into the Upper Carp River Gorge. At the river itself as easy ford puts you on the west bank at the junction with Government Peak Trail. Head north along this trail to reach a pair of scenic backcountry campsites in a quarter mile and M-107 in 2 miles. Head south to first pass Trap Falls, and then an Adirondack shelter in less than a half mile.

Summit Peak Tower Trail
Summit Peak Road To South Mirror Lake Trail
Distance: *0.5 mile to Summit Peak Tower*
1 mile to South Mirror Lake Trail
Highest Point: *1,958 feet*
Hiking Time: *1 hour*

From the picnic area and parking lot at the end of Summit Peak Road, a wide trail makes a steady ascent towards the park's highest peak. Planking and long staircases assist you in climbing the 258 feet to the tower, but it's still a steady climb, especially for older visitors and young children.

Within 0.4 mile you arrive at a viewing platform with benches. From the deck you are rewarded with a good view of the park's rugged interior including the marshes that the Little Carp River passes through. The trail continues to climb and shortly you arrive at the 40-foot high, 60-step tower at the top of Summit Peak, third highest point in Michigan at 1,958 feet.

It is debatable how extensive the view from the tower is, but on a clear day some claim to view the ski flying ramp on top of Copper Peak to the northwest. Most visitors have a hard time spotting Lake Superior and the small bit of Mirror Lake's shoreline much less Wisconsin or the Apostle Islands. The view is still impressive, however, as the ruggedness of the Porkies is as evident here as any overlook in the park.

The second half of the trail is a straight drop off the peak, with some sections being extremely steep. Caution should be used and the switchbacks followed as you descend a half mile from the peak to South Mirror Lake Trail, 1.2 miles from the lake itself. By heading south (right) at the junction, you could turn the outing into a 3-mile loop by following South Mirror Lake Trail as it gently descends a mile to Summit Peak Road. The loop would be completed by hiking up the road to your vehicle.

🏃 Beaver Creek and Lily Pond Trails

Round Trip from Summit Peak Road
Distance: *5 miles*
Highest Point: *1,700 feet*
Hiking Time: *3 to 4 hours*

These two trails plus a portion of Little Carp River Trail form a pleasant half-day hike along a route that is scenic but not nearly as heavily traveled during the summer as the Escarpment or the Mirror Lake trails. Throw in the mile that people with only one vehicle have to hike along Summit Peak Road from one trailhead to other and this outing is a 6-mile day.

It is an easier hike if you start with Beaver Creek Trail at the parking area at the end of Summit Peak Road. Keep in mind, however, parking is very limited here and the lot is often filled on a clear day. If that's the case, consider parking at the Lily Pond Trailhead and beginning with the park road.

Beaver Creek Trail
Distance: 2 miles to Lily Pond

Beaver Creek begins near the toilet building, wanders into the maple forest and immediately arrives at second trailhead posted where the foot path swings away from an old logging road. The trail is clearly mark and from here crosses a small stream and then makes rapid descent from the Summit Peak area into a gorge formed by the so called Beaver Creek, though it is not labeled on

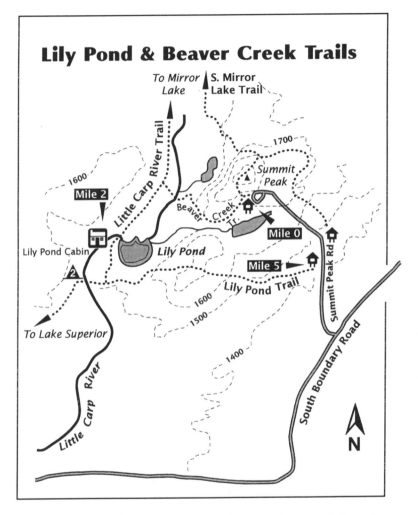

Lily Pond & Beaver Creek Trails

To Mirror Lake

S. Mirror Lake Trail

1700

Little Carp River Trail

1600

Summit Peak

Mile 2

Beaver Creek Tr.

Mile 0

Lily Pond Cabin

Lily Pond

Mile 5

2

Lily Pond Trail

Summit Peak Rd

1600

1500

To Lake Superior

1400

Little Carp River

South Boundary Road

Little Carp River

N

maps. This downhill walk is an impressive stretch as you follow the stream through the steep-sided and boulder-strewn gorge.

Eventually you bottom out and swing away from the creek to pass the old logging road once again and arrive at the extensive marsh area surrounding Little Carp River. A bridge and then planking with a small knob of dry ground in the middle provides dry footing across the marsh to the junction of Little Carp River Trail

The bridge over Little Carp River at Lily Pond.

on the other side. But take your time crossing for the opportunities to sight wildlife, including beavers, are very good here.

At the posted junction, Mirror Lake is 1.5 miles east along Little Carp River Trail while Lily Pond is a a very short mile to the west. Heading west, the trail is a level walk through a mix of hardwoods and pines with an occasional wet area to step through before you break out at the impressive bridge across Little Carp River. The huge wooden structure features a bench in the middle angled towards the view of Lily Pond and the surrounding ridges. The bench and the view make the bridge a great place for an extended break or lunch.

Lily Pond Trail
Distance: 3 miles

Little Carp River Trail departs into an impressive stand of white pine and in less than a half mile reaches the posted junction with Lily Pond Trail. Continue with the Little Carp River Trail and you will reach Lake Superior in 8.5 miles.

Head east on Lily Pond Trail to return to Summit Peak Road in 2.5 miles. You immediately pass a pair of old tree stump chairs that have been cleverly carved with a chainsaw and now are padded with green moss. Who says park rangers aren't creative? Shortly beyond them the trail begins its ascent out of Little Carp River valley.

The climb is gentle and along the way you move from pines into a virgin stand of maple and beech and pass some impressively large trunks. Thimbleberry patches will also begin appearing and if your timing is right you will be stopping at every splash of red along the trail. There is one steep but short pitch a mile from Little Carp River Trail that ends with the high point of 1,720 feet where a bench has been built.

Once over the top, the trail makes a steady descent for a half mile to cross a stream at 1,500 feet and enters a towering stand of hemlock. The mile-long descent to Summit Park Road at 1,400 feet is much more gentle and you will cross one last stream just before breaking out at the parking lot.

GREENSTONE FALLS ACCESS TRAIL
Little Carp Road To Greenstone Falls
Map on page 82
Distance: *0.75 miles*
Highest Point: *1,300 feet*
Hiking Time: *30 minutes*

This trail is used by many to gain quick access to both Section 17 and Greenstone Falls cabins but also makes for an easy round-trip dayhike of 1.5 miles pass several cascades. The trailhead is posted at the end of Little Carp River Road, reached 9 miles from Presque Isle or 16 miles from the Visitor Center.

The trail departs along the river bank and within 100 feet comes to Overlooked Falls, a pair of cascades with a total drop 10 feet. The second one is quite scenic as it is split in the middle by a huge boulder. The trail stays briefly on top of the small gorge the Little Carp River cuts here and then descends into it via a set of steps.

At the bottom you cross the river at a massive log jam where one huge pine has been cut into a foot bridge. The trail climbs out of the gorge on the other side to the junction with the Little Carp River Trail. Greenstone Falls is a mere 100 yards west along the Little Carp and is a scenic spot. Set in a small gorge, the cascade features a 15-foot wide veil that tumbles down a series of rock steps and small boulders. Continue west along Little Carp River Trail to reach **Greenstone Falls Cabin** in another 100 yards and **Section 17 Cabin** in less than a half mile

East and West River Trails

Round Trip From Presque Isle Day-use Area
Distance: *2 miles*
Highest Point: *700 feet*
Hiking Time: *1 hour*

The East River Trail and the West River Trail are actually two separate paths but when combined, as they usually are, they form another scenic loop in the Porkies and the best trek for families with young children. The outing packs in adventure, stands of virgin hemlock, waterfalls and great scenery almost every step of the way along a loop that is only 2 miles long. This could very well be the best short trail Michigan has to offer.

It is certainly one of the most spectacular spots in our state. In its final mile before emptying into Lake Superior, the Presque Isle descends more than 100 feet and in doing so has carved a rugged and steep-sided gorge and filled it with waterfalls.

Beginning in the park's Presque Isle Day-use Area, you waste no time in getting to the river. The trail immediately turns into a long stairway that leads you down to the Presque Isle and across the rushing water on an impressive swing bridge. From the middle of the bridge, it is an incredible view up stream. Presque Isle is by far the largest river to flow through the Porkies and its current is

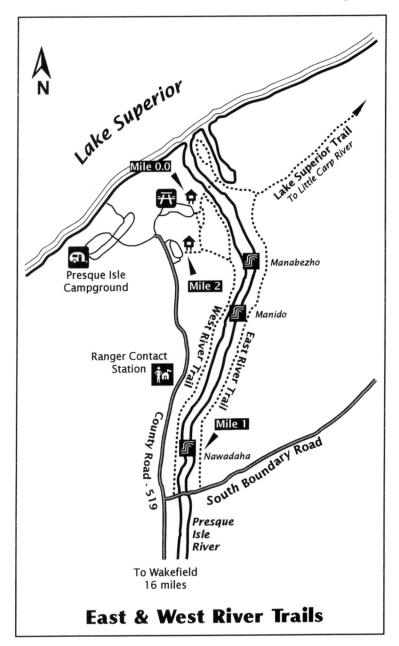

N

Lake Superior

Mile 0.0

Lake Superior Trail
To Little Carp River

Presque Isle
Campground

Manabezho

Mile 2

West River Trail

East River Trail

Manido

Ranger Contact
Station

Mile 1

County Road - 519

Nawadaha

South Boundary Road

Presque
Isle
River

To Wakefield
16 miles

East & West River Trails

Backpackers cross the Presque Isle River at the west end of the Lake Superior Trail.

so strong that the whirlpool swirl of the water has carved perfect half-circles in the bedrock below you.

What appears on maps as a peninsula on the other side of the bridge is actually an island in the mouth of the river with a dry channel on one side that becomes flooded during high water. Trails cross the island to Lake Superior.

The marked route leads you to the dry channel on the east side, an intriguing spot. Crossing the channel you climb across layers of shale with a small waterfall in the background before reaching the other side of the gorge. Here the East River Trail begins with a steep climb out, topping off at the posted junction with the 16-mile long Lake Superior Trail. The East Trail heads south, climbing along the edge of the gorge and over masses of roots from the towering stand of virgin hemlock, white pine and cedar. The trees are impressive here, but the walk can be challenging at times.

Eventually the trail descends to a bench overlooking Manabezho and Manido falls, a pair thundering cascades just down river from each other. The first is Manabezho Falls, the most impressive cascade along the river. The falls make a 20 to 25-foot thundering drop over a rock ledge and create a heavy mist and a blanket of form. Another 100 yards upstream is Manido Falls, which descend 25 feet over a gradually declining set of rock ledges.

The trail stays on the edge of the gorge and you can view a series of cascades for the next half mile until you arrive at Nawadaha Falls where the river tumbles 15 feet over a series of rock steps. At this point the trail swings away from the river until you break out at the South Boundary Road. Just on the other side of the bridge, you quickly leave the pavement and return to a needle-carpeted path to the West River Trail which leads through an impressive stand of hemlock.

The west side is a much easier hike. You stay near the river and for a half mile weave through the trees, passing Nawadaha Falls a second time. Eventually the trail dips down to the water itself for a unusual angle of the river. Looking down stream all you see is a flat placid surface of the Presque Isle. Hidden from view is Manido Falls. Imagine Indians paddling this stretch for the first time to be suddenly conforted with the 25-foot cascade.

Planking leads up the side of the gorge to the trail's impressive boardwalk section where large viewing areas put you right above Manido Falls and then Manabezho. You are so close you can feel their cooling mist on a hot afternoon. It is so impressive, you're disappointed when you soon return to the stairway that leads back to the day-use area.

A pair of snowshoers enjoy the deep powder found in the Porkies throughout the winter.

10 WINTER IN THE PORKIES

To see that the Porcupine Mountains is not Boyne Highlands, Crystal Mountain or any of Michigan's other glitzy ski resorts, all you have do is look inside the chalet.

Crockpots plugged in along the wall are slowly cooking lunch while the families are skiing outside. In the middle, there are a dozen people sitting around the open fireplace roasting hotdogs on sticks and in the corner somebody's four-year-old just climbed into her sleeping bag for a mid-afternoon nap.

Better yet, take a look from the top. From the Eastern Summit you see the frozen Upper Peninsula shoreline all the way to Ontonagon, 20 miles away. From the Western Summit it is nothing but the endless blue of Lake Superior. The lake is so close there is a sensation when skiing that you will hit water before you hit the bottom.

No matter where you look, it is pretty obvious; downhill skiing in the Porkies is unique. So is cross country skiing, snowshoeing or just spending a night in a rustic cabin... a quarter mile from your car.

If you like the Porkies in the summer and are charmed by the mountains during autumn colors, you will be intrigued with the park during the winter when the snow is so deep it is chest high the minute your step out of your snowshoes. There is a different beauty to the land during February when Lake Superior's shoreline is a gallery of ice sculptures and the boughs of each pine are struggling under a layer of snow.

There is also a different crowd at the park; a very small one. You still have to reserve a cabin in advance, but lines at the chair lifts are as rare as spring weather in March, and cross country skiing is a solitary pursuit into the woods.

 What's Available

Traditionally winter arrives at the Porkies in mid-December and lasts to the first of April. At this time of the year the staff concentrates its activities and services to what is referred to as the Porcupine Mountains Winter Recreation Area in the northeast corner of the park. Access is strictly along M-107 from Silver City as South Boundary Road becomes part of a snowmobile route. The park road is not plowed beyond the entrance to alpine ski area, which makes the Lake of the Clouds Escarpment the most scenic snowmobile destination in the state.

The Visitor Center is closed during the winter, and all backcountry permits and cabins rentals should be arranged at the park headquarters. One mile west of the Union Bay Campground is the alpine ski area with the downhill slopes, Chalet, ski rental and a large, two-tier parking lot. The parking lot is also used by cross country skiers as nearby are the trailheads for the River and Union Spring run and the Deer Yard Trail.

Along with downhill slopes and 42 kilometers of groomed Nordic tracks, three rustic cabins are available for use during the winter. None of the other cabins or the campgrounds are open from December through March.

Alpine Skiing

The Porkies have a lot of things of which no other downhill ski area can boast. For starters, it is surrounded by 60,000 acres of designated wilderness, and since it is a state park its lift tickets are the lowest of any comparable ski area in the state. Children 12 years and under, ski free and adults pay about half what they would pay at any major resort in the Lower Peninsula.

Few resorts in Michigan have the Porkies' powder. Warm air passing over frigid Lake Superior picks up moisture and deposits it as powder snow, up to 20 feet in a season. Winter temperatures are often 10 to 20 degrees warmer than inland ski areas.

Downhill skiers pause to admire the view of Lake Superior..

The Porkies have a vertical drop of 600 feet which is one of the highest in the Midwest. The 11 miles of ski slopes covers 80 acres within the 320-acre alpine area. The 14 runs are served by a handle tow on the Bunny Slope, a double chair lift to the Western Summit and a T-bar lift and a triple chair lift to the Eastern Summit, a ride of 2,800 feet. Total lift capacity is 3,500 skiers per hour.

Four runs; Ojibway, Cut-Over, Cuyahoga and Agate Run, are rated for advance\expert skiers with Agate Run and Cuyahoga departing from the Eastern Summit and extending the length of the mountain.

There are seven intermediate runs, including Superior View which is accessed from the double chair lift and lives up to its name with a spectacular views of the lake's frozen shoreline much of the way. Another intermediate slope, Ridge Run, is so scenic there is an observation deck with benches where skiers stop on a clear day to enjoy the view of the forested shoreline to Silver City.

Beyond the Bunny Slope, located downhill from the Chalet, the other beginner runs are Sunset and Hidden Valley. Sunset is

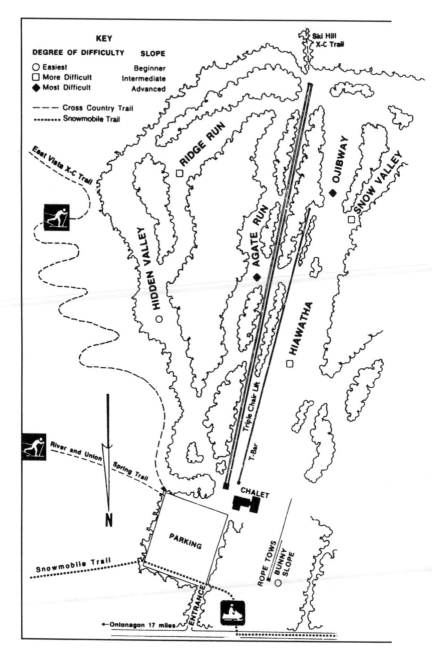

KEY

DEGREE OF DIFFICULTY   **SLOPE**

○ Easiest   Beginner
□ More Difficult   Intermediate
◆ Most Difficult   Advanced

— — — Cross Country Trail
········· Snowmobile Trail

Ski Hill X-C Trail

East Vista X-C Trail

RIDGE RUN

OJIBWAY

SNOW VALLEY

HIDDEN VALLEY

AGATE RUN

HIAWATHA

Triple Chair Lift

T-Bar

River and Union   Spring Trail

N

CHALET

PARKING

ROPE TOWS
BUNNY SLOPE

Snowmobile Trail

ENTRANCE

←Ontonagon 17 miles

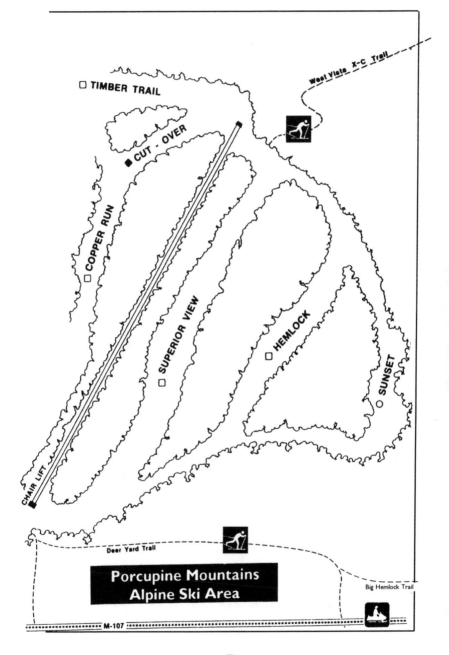

TIMBER TRAIL

West Vista X-C Trail

CUT - OVER

COPPER RUN

SUPERIOR VIEW

HEMLOCK

SUNSET

CHAIR LIFT

Deer Yard Trail

Porcupine Mountains Alpine Ski Area

Big Hemlock Trail

M-107

longest run on the mountain at 6,000 feet and reached from the double chair. Hidden Valley is a three-quarter mile, round-the-hill run best suited for advanced beginners. It also features Lake Superior views, but at the beginning starts out with some narrow curves and sudden drops.

At the base is the Chalet, a large A-frame lodge with three fireplaces, food service, lockers, modern restrooms, and a glass wall in the main lounge that overlooks the Hiawatha Run. Inside is a rental service for both downhill and Nordic equipment, a ski shop and National Ski Patrol first aid services. The downhill ski area is open daily from 9 a.m. to 5 p.m. and lift tickets are purchased inside the Chalet.

 # Cross Country Skiing

Throughout the winter, the state park grooms and maintains 42-kilometers of Nordic ski trails or basically a 26-mile network of four main loops. The tracks are double set, posted with locator maps at major junctions and rated from "Easiest" and "More Difficult" to "Most Difficult".

The most practical place to start any cross country trip is the Chalet where nearby are three trailheads providing access to the Nonesuch Trail to the east, Big Hemlock Trail to the west or Deer Yard and Superior Loop south of M-107 to the shores of Lake Superior. For the quickest access to the heart of the trail system or to enjoy the spectacular panoramas at East and West Vistas, cross country skiers can purchase a one-trip tow ticket. The ticket can be used on the either the triple chair to reach the Eastern Summit or the double chair to the Western Summit from which a variety of trails then quickly descend the back side of the mountain.

The easiest trail is Superior Loop which can be handled by most beginners and includes a view of the ice formations along Lake Superior. The most challenging route is Big Hemlock and Union Spring Trails, a 12-mile, 19-kilometer loop that is an all-day ski for most skiers.

Skiers warm-up at the fire place in the park chalet.

 ## Superior Loop

Distance: *1.5 miles/2.4 km*
Rating: *Easiest*

Most of the groomed routes within the park involve some steep downhill runs which to many beginners and intermediate skiers translates to take-off-your-skies-and-walk-down the slopes. These are, after all, the Porcupine Mountains. But, luckily for families with young skiers, not all trails are that difficult.

Superior Loop is one of the most scenic ski trails in the Porkies as well as the shortest and easiest to handle. Maybe that's why it is trailhead is located next to the Bunny Slope.

You no more than depart the tow rope area and enter the woods when you emerge at M-107 and are forced to high step it across the pavement. On the other side you enter a hardwood

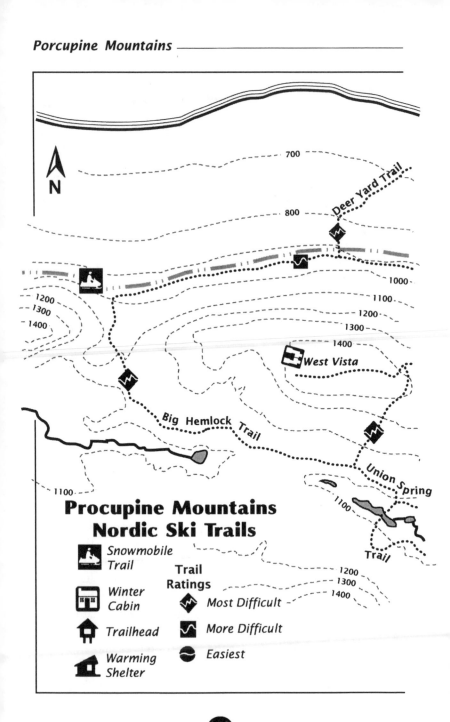

700

Deer Yard Trail

800

1000

1100
1200
1300

1200
1300
1400

West Vista

1400

Big Hemlock Trail

Union Spring

1100

1100

Trail

1200
1300
1400

Procupine Mountains
Nordic Ski Trails

Snowmobile Trail

Winter Cabin

Trailhead

Warming Shelter

Trail Ratings

Most Difficult

More Difficult

Easiest

N

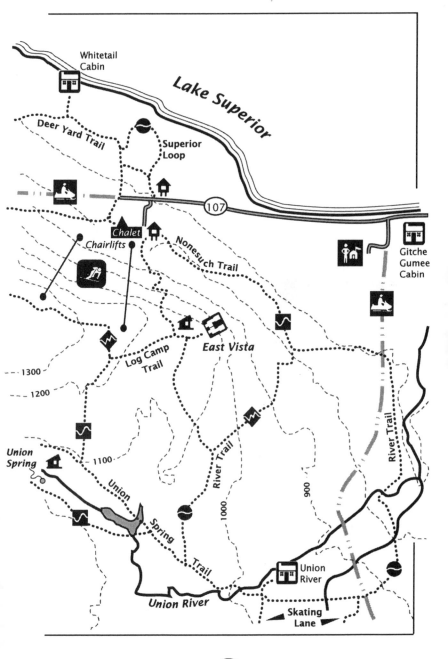

forest thick with paper birch that is especially enchanting on the cloudless day and continue on a gentle downhill run towards the Lake Superior. You pass two posted junctions with the second one heading west along the Deer Yard Trail, then emerge at the edge of the forest for a view of Lake Superior.

What a view! The lake is open and a deeper shade of blue than the sky but the shoreline is usually piled high with ice and blanketed in white by the last snowfall. It is pretty evident from the tracks in the snow that most skiers cannot resist departing the trail and striding across the ice for a better view of the huge bergs, ice caves and frozen arches that are formed during the long Upper Peninsula winter. *BUT BE CAREFUL TO AVOID SLIPPING IN!*

From the lakeshore you circle back and encounter your only steep slope on the run. But it's short and any mishap is done with the knowledge that you will soon be back at the Chalet, kicking off your boots and roasting marshmallows at the open fireplace with a dozen other children and parents.

Deer Yard Trail

Distance: *3 miles/4.8 km*
Rating: *Most Difficult*

Deer Yard is a 4-mile loop that is rated "Most Difficult" primarily because of a wicked downhill run toward Lake Superior at its west end. Thrill seekers will want to ski Deer Yard in a clockwise direction beginning at the Bunny Slope Trailhead. More cautious skiers will take a counter clockwise direction, beginning with the segment that the trail shares with the Superior Loop. At the second posted junction you head west, pass through an open marsh area, and then quickly arrive at the signposted spur to Whitetail Cabin, an eight-bunk unit overlooking Lake Superior.

Deer Yard continues west through a young forest of predominantly paper birch. It then enters a growth of stately hemlock and swings south to begin its steep climb to M-107. If you are coming in the other direction this is a twisting, turning, rapid descent where you fly past huge pine trees. If you are climbing this section, take heart. At least you have more time to admire the timber.

Eventually you emerge at M-107, cross it and pick up the trail on the other side. The final leg back to the chalet parallels the park road from above, gently descending most of the way until you are again mingling with the kid skiers back at the bunny slope.

Nonesuch & River Trails

Distance: *7 miles/11.2 km*
Rating: *More difficult*

This is a scenic run, a 7-mile (11.2 kilometer) loop that can be handled by most intermediate skiers without too much difficultly. You can also turn this trip into an overnight adventure by reserving the Union River Cabin, conveniently located roughly halfway.

In the southeast corner of the ski area parking is a trailhead with a posted map, displaying both the start of the Nonesuch Trail and the East Vista Trail. Adventurous skiers can follow the East Vista route to the scenic overlook and then return to the River and NonesuchTrails. Keep in mind this segment is rated "Most Difficult" and is a tough climb from the parking lot.

Nonesuch Trail is somewhat easier but still involves quite a bit of climbing in the beginning. You no more than enter the forest when you are faced with the first hill. The slope is steep, it is long and at the base it could also be wet in late winter. Signs will warn skiers coming from the other direction of both the steepness and the possibility of a wet trail.

Several more ascents are made and then you are rewarded with a long downhill run and from there it is a couple of strides to the first posted junction. To the east (left) the trail heads for South Boundary Road, a snowmobile route in the winter. To the south (right) is River Trail, which allows for the quickest route to Union River Cabin. The trail is a relatively level run through a hardwood forest where within a mile you arrive at the posted junction with the trail from East Vista. You remain on the level run and within another mile arrive at a posted junction.

Head west (right) to follow the Union Spring Trail. The River

Porcupine Mountains grooms a 42-kilometer system of trails with a set of double tracks for cross country skiers in the winter.

Trail, however, continues east (left) where you quickly descend a hill, cross gurgling Cleveland Creek and then climb to the posted junction to the Union River cabin. From the cabin spur it is a half mile until you reach the posted parking lot for hikers and then another stride or two and you are crossing South Boundary Road.

On the other side, the trail is posted with a map and a "More Difficult" diamond, but in this direction it is not a hard ski as you begin with a gentle downhill run through a forest that is a pleasant mix of leafless hardwoods and older pines. There are a pair of steep slopes and from the second one you descend to the Union River and a vehicle bridge that is used in the summer by campers.

Once across the bridge you immediately re-enter the woods and begin the most beautiful stretch of the trail. For the next 20 to 30 minutes you ski between the Union River and towering wooded bluff on the other side. Here you'll usually find the snow deep and the creek open even during the coldest winters. This wooded area is often a quiet sanctuary from the winds off Lake Superior. Eventually the pines give way to a stand of all hardwoods and you quickly emerge at South Boundary Road for the second time. Look both ways before crossing, snowmobilers seem to come out of nowhere.

On the other side you merge into a portion of the nature trail from the Visitor's Center, the reason for the interpretive signs. You eventually cross Jamison Creek and then come to the posted junction with Nonesuch Trail that you first passed from the parking lot. Head north (right) to return to the Chalet, only this time most of the skiing will be downhill.

Big Hemlock & Union Spring Trails

Distance: *12 miles/19 km*
Rating: *Most Difficult*

These two trails form the longest groomed loop in the park, a 12-mile (19 kilometer) ski into the backcountry of the Porkies. This is a day-long adventure for most skiers and if the weather is nice many plan an extended break or a meal at Union Spring. If you want to shorten the loop to approximately a 5-mile ski, purchase a single ride tow ticket and descend the backside of the mountain from the cross over trail nearest West Vista. But be forewarned, it's a steep run. *Eeeehaa!!!*

The first 3 miles of the loop share the same route with Nonesuch and River Trails, beginning at the trailhead in the southeast corner of the ski parking lot. However instead of heading east (left) at the third posted junction, head west (right) along a wide, double track trail to quickly arrive at a posted junction to Union Spring. The groomed trail bypasses the springs, but the side trail splits to the south and is normally not double tracked. You quickly ski past the frozen surface of Union Pond and then enter the woods. Here you will find a narrow trail that winds between the trees...no place to skate here. You ski around the pond and then skirt its west end to arrive at the spring itself. The observation deck may be heaped with snow, but most of the spring stays open during the water and you can still lean over the railing to view the bubbling sand at the bottom. There is a bench nearby and the area makes for a quiet and scenic spot for an extended break if you can manage to stay warm long enough.

Beyond the spring, the run resumes as a narrow and winding trail through the thick woods. A number of times you dip into lowlying areas that might still be wet before finally swinging to the north and crossing a meadow ringed by trees. In winter, this is an extremely scenic opening and just beyond it you return to the groomed track.

Heading west the loop continues with a long climb that tops off at the posted junction with spur from the West Vista. Beyond the junction the trail is named Big Hemlock on park maps and begins with a spirited downhill run. A climb of another long hill tops off in a stand of towering pines, many of them virgin hemlock.

Big Hemlock Trail remains in the pines for another stretch of scenic skiing and eventually you reach its junction with Government Peak Trail, posted with mileage for hikers. Head north (right) and in the next mile you will climb through the hardwoods, pass hiker's junctions to the Overlook Trail again, continue to the Escarpment Trail, and then begin a wicked run downhill. Be Careful

Backcountry skiers depart the Union River Cabin in February.

as you could end up flying onto M-107 which snowmobilers follow to the Lake of the Clouds.

The final 2.5 miles begins by following M-107 but twice dips into the woods to follow a trail above the road. Eventually you pass the posted junction to the Deer Yard Loop and then begin a gentle downhill run to the Chalet, ending up at the Bunny Slope.

🎿 East And West Vistas

What could easily be the best panoramas in Michigan seen from cross country skis are the East and West Vistas at the top of the park's alpine area, especially the West Vista. Both are an enjoyable trips up if you first purchase a single ride tow ticket at the Chalet.

Utilizing the chairs with Nordic equipment is easy even if you're lugging a backpack. The chair operators will slow down the lift or stop it completely to allow you enough time to climb on at the bottom and slide off at the top.

East Vista: Begin on the triple chair and from the ramp on top head right toward the beginning of the Hidden Valley Run. A sign marks where the cross country trail departs into the woods and a yellow caution sign tips you off what lies ahead. The first section is an extremely steep run where many skiers end up doing little more than snow plowing and praying.

The run ends at the first of three junctions to the overlook. Head east along Log Camp Trail (left) for the vista. The trail straight ahead is the middle route off the backside of the mountain and posted "Most Difficult." The vista trail follows the gently rolling crest of the ridge and quickly arrives at the second posted junction with a downhill route back to the parking lot that is also rated "Most Difficult".

The third junction is posted with a sign to East Vista, and you quickly emerge from the trees to climb an open knob. Here you gaze east to view the Lake Superior shoreline to Silver City and beyond on a clear day while to the southeast is the copper mine.

The quickest way to return to the Chalet is to retrace your steps to the second junction but that involves a challenging downhill run down to the parking lot. The easiest way is to descend the backside of the hill from the East Vista spur along Log Camp Trail, which makes a much milder descent from the high alpine area. You will bottom out at a posted junction with the River Trail and from there head north (left) to loop back to the ski area parking lot.

West Vista: Begin on the double chair and at the top head west (right) to the posted cross country trailhead near the start of the Hemlock downhill slope. You quickly come to another posted junction. Continue west (right) to reach the vista and you will soon find the trail begins a long and somewhat steep climb. You top out to continue along the rolling crest of the ridge until the groomed trail ends in half a mile.

Pathway signs will lead you to the overlook as this section is shared with hikers during the summer. You continue to climb through the trees until you break out the opening that is the West

Vista. You can see Lake Superior from here along with the Upper Carp River Valley and the entire Escarpment. The view is best during the winter when the trees are leafless and you can see a sprawling valley that appears to be enclosed by a pair of mountain ranges. There isn't another panorama like this one in all of Michigan and maybe the entire Midwest.

From the West Vista you can follow the route down the backside of the mountain at the second posted junction; then ski the remaining 5 miles of the Big Hemlock Trail. Keep in mind this is by far the most challenging downhill portion of the park's ski trail network. An easier return is to retrace your steps back to the alpine area and follow the Timber Trail (downhill ski run) to the East Vista trailhead. From here you can return one of two ways (see above section). Of course, if you know how to telemark then you can always follow the downhill skiers to the Chalet.

 Lake of the Clouds

Distance: *6 miles/9.5 km one way*
Rating: *More difficult*

Skiers also follow the unplowed portion of M-107 to the Lake of the Clouds overlook, a spot that is as an enchanting in winter as it is in summer. The skiing is easy, but be aware that this is a popular side trip with snowmobilers. For the more adventurous, a return along the Escarpment Trail is challenging but the views are well worth the extra energy spent breaking a trail.

Cabins

Three cabins within the park have been specially built for winter use and are the only ones that can be reserved from December through March. They should be reserved well in advance as they are popular destinations for cross country skiers.

Gitche Gumee: This cabin is just off M-107 and a mere 20-yard walk from where you park the car. The eight-bunk cabin is handicapped accessible but does not adjoin the Nordic trail system.

Whitetail: This eight-bunk is a mile ski from the Chalet along the east half of the Deer Yard Trail, an easy run. The cabin sits on a low bluff overlooking Lake Superior, and the ice formations along its shoreline and provide access to the rest of the trail network.

Union River: This unit is located halfway around the 7-mile River Trail from the Chalet. By purchasing a one-ride tow ticket and taking the triple chair to the East Vista you can reduce the first day to approximately a 2.5-mile ski and add a sense of adventure with a ride to the top of the downhill slopes. The cabin is set along the Union River, a stream that is usually open throughout the winter. Like Whitetail, the cabin is well positioned away from the groomed trail for a secluded setting.

 Snowshoeing

The Porcupine Mountains draws almost a half million visitors a year, the vast majority campers and hikers during the summer. A large number also come in the winter to downhill or cross country ski. But the most unusual time in Michigan's largest state park is the April snowshoe season.

When the park is devoid of any other visitor, a small but hardy group arrives for one of the great wilderness adventures in Michigan; skiing and snowshoeing miles across this rugged land-scape to be the first people to use the park's network of backcountry cabins.

The park has 16 cabins but only the three newest units are rented year-round. The rest are too isolated to maintain in the winter so they are closed December through March. Come April all the cabins are available but the snow is still there, more than three feet of it in the woods, almost as much covering South Boundary Road and M-107, the access roads into the park.

Thus what is a 2- or 3-mile hike to a cabin in the summer becomes a major expedition in April that first involves skiing the

A snowshoer packs along her cross country skis for a stay at Section 17 Cabin in early April. Many of the park's cabins are rented during the April snowshoe season.

access roads to the trails and then snowshoeing to the shelter you rented for the night.

Although a few cabins, like Speakers, are a trek of less than a mile in the spring, the majority are much longer. Some, like the three cabins at Mirror Lake, make for a one-way journey of 10 to 12 miles putting them out of reach of most recreational snowshoers. One of the best cabins for this adventure is Section 17 Cabin, a one-way trek of seven miles.

The heavy backpacks are tough to avoid on this adventure. You not only have to be equipped for both skiing and snowshoeing but be prepared for a time of year when you worry about frostbite and sunburn. You pack in mittens and sunglasses, a wool hat for the nights, suntan lotion for those bright almost blinding, 60-degree afternoons.

Often South Boundary Road is an easy ski, a well packed route thanks to snowmobilers who travel it throughout the winter. The trails, however, are often too narrow, the trees too numerous, to negotiate with cross country skis, the reason for the snowshoes.

The key to this unusual adventure is using expedition snowshoes with enough surface space to support both you and your pack and with crampons on the bindings to tackle icy slopes. You also need to book the cabins in advance, sometimes as much as a year. The snowshoe season is short, generally three weeks, and the cabins most people are capable of reaching are limited to a handful on the fringe of the park; Speakers, Greenstone Falls, Section 17 or Lake of the Clouds.

Is it worth pink toes and sunburnt cheeks?

Without question. The April scenery of high snowbanks, towering hemlocks and gushing streams is intriguing. The waterfalls are stunning. In the end the most intriguing aspect of the trip wasn't being the first ones out here, but the only ones.

Map and Trail Index

Appendix

Backpacking Itineraries

The following is suggested backpacking itineraries with both daily and total mileage for various trips into the Porcupine Mountains Wilderness State Park. Each outing is a loop to eliminate the need for two vehicles. The treks are also arranged with short hikes the first day, the day most visitors arrive at the park, and follow the easiest direction of travel.

All backpackers must first register before entering the backcountry at either the Visitor Center or the park headquarters off of South Boundary Road. There is a nightly fee for trailside camping and all camps must be a quarter mile from any cabin, scenic area such as rivers, Adirondack shelter or road.

Six-day Outing	Mileage
Lake Superior Trailhead on M-107	0.0
1st Day: Lake Superior Trail	
to Buckshot Landing	2.5
2nd Day: Lake Superior Trail	
to Mouth of Little Carp River	7.5
3rd Day: Little Carp River Trail	
to Greenstone Falls Area	6.0
4th Day: Little Carp River Trail	
to Mirror Lake	5.5
5th Day: Government Peak Trail	
to Trap Falls area	6.5
6th Day: Escarpment Trail	
to M-107 Trailhead	7.0
TOTAL	35.0

Five-day Outing	**Mileage**
Lake Superior Trailhead on M-107	0.0
1st Day: Lake Superior Trail	
to Buckshot Landing	2.5
2nd Day: Lake Superior Trail	
to Mouth of Little Carp River	7.5
3rd Day: Little Carp River Trail	
to Greenstone Falls Area	6.0
4th Day: Little Carp River Trail	
to Mirror Lake	5.5
5th Day: North Mirror Lake Trail	
to M-107 Trailhead	5.0
TOTAL	26.5

Four-day Outing	
Trailhead on Little Carp River Road	0.0
1st Day: Little Carp River Trail	
to Lily Pond	3.0
2nd Day: Correction Line Trail	
to Big Carp River shelter	5.5
3rd Day: Big Carp River Trail	
to Mouth of Little Carp River	5.0
4th Day: Little Carp River Trail	
to Trailhead	6.0
TOTAL	19.5

Four-day Outing	
Lake Superior Trailhead on M-107	0.0
1st Day: Lake Superior Trail	
to Buckshot Landing	2.5
2nd Day: Lake Superior Trail	
to Mouth of Big Carp River	6.5
3rd Day: Big Carp River Trail	
to Mirror Lake	7.0
4th Day: North Mirror Lake Trail	
to M-107 Trailhead	5.0
TOTAL	21.0

Three-day Outing   **Mileage**

	Mileage
Trailhead on Little Carp River Road	0.0
1st Day: Little Carp River Trail	
to Cross Trail Junction	1.0
2nd Day: Cross Trail	
to Mouth of Little Carp River	6.0
3rd Day: Little Carp River Trail	
to Trailhead	6.0
TOTAL	13.0

Three-day Outing

South Mirror Lake Trailhead	0.0
1st Day: South Mirror Lake Trail	
to Mirror Lake	2.5
2nd Day: North Mirror Lake Trail	
to Big Carp River shelter	9.0
3rd Day: Correction Line Trail	
to Summit Peak Road Trailhead	5.5
TOTAL	17.0

Three-day Outing   **Mileage**

	Mileage
Government Peak Trailhead on M-107	0.0
1st Day: Government Peak Trail	
to Trap Falls Area	2.0
2nd Day: Government Peak Trail	
to Mirror Lake	6.0
Third Day: North Mirror Lake Trail	
to M-107 Trailhead	8.0
TOTAL	16.0

Three-day Outing   **Mileage**

	Mileage
Lake Superior Trailhead on M-107	0.0
1st Day: Lake Superior Trail	
to Buckshot Landing	2.5
2nd Day: Lake Superior Trail	
to Shining Falls area	8.0
3rd Day: Big Carp River Trail	
to Lake of the Clouds Overlook	8.5
TOTAL	19.0

Two-day Outing
South Mirror Lake Trailhead	0.0
1st Day: South Mirror Lake Trail to Mirror Lake	2.5
2nd Day: Little Carp River Trail to Trailhead via Lily Pond	6.5
TOTAL	9.0

Two-day Outing
Government Peak Trailhead on M-107	0.0
1st Day: Government Peak Trail to Trap Falls Area	2.0
2nd Day: Backtrack via Overlook Trail to M-107 Trailhead	4.5
TOTAL	6.5

Additional Sources of Information

The following are the addresses and phone numbers to a variety of organizations and agencies that can assist in planning any trip to Upper Peninsula:

Porcupine Mountains Wilderness State Park
412 South Boundary Rd.
Ontonagon, MI 49953
☎ (906) 885-5275
Contact the park for information about backpacking, cabin rentals, campground reservations or winter activities.

The Michigan Department of Natural Resources
Parks Division
P.O. Box 30028
Lansing, MI 48909
☎ (517) 373-1270
For other information about other Michigan state parks including campground facilities and hiking opportunities.

Ottawa National Forest
E6248 US-2
Ironwood, MI 49938
☎ (906) 932-1330
The Porkies are practically surrounded by Ottawa National Forest, which offers a wide range of hiking and backpacking opportunities as well as many rustic campgrounds.

Ontonagon Tourism
P.O. Box 266
Ontonagon, MI 49953
☎ (906) 884-4735
The county office can provide information on lodging and campgrounds just outside the Porkies.

Upper Peninsula Travel & Recreation Association
P.O. Box 400
Iron Mountain, MI 49801
☎ (906) 774-5480
    or (800) 562-7134
For additional information on lodging, attractions and campgrounds through out the Upper Peninsula.

Michigan Travel Bureau
P.O. Box 30226
Lansing, MI 48909
☎ (800) 543-2937
Contact the bureau for a state highway map or travel information for anywhere in Michigan.

About The Author

Jim DuFresne is an outdoor writer based in Clarkston, Mich. and author of 15 wilderness\travel guidebooks. His books cover areas from Alaska and New Zealand to Michigan's own Isle Royale National Park. His syndicated column, *Kidventures* appear in daily newspapers throughout Michigan.

DuFresne is a journalism graduate from Michigan State University and the former outdoors and sports editor of the Juneau Empire, where in 1980 he became the first Alaskan sportswriter to ever win a national award from Associated Press.

Along with *Porcupine Mountains Wilderness State Park* (Pegg Legg Publications), DuFresne's other recent titles include *Wild Michigan* (Northword Press), a look at the state's wilderness areas, *60 Hikes In Michigan's Lower Peninsula* (Backcountry Publications), *Isle Royale National Park : Foot Trails & Water Routes* (Mountaineer-Books), *Tramping In New Zealand* (Lonely Planet) and *Alaska: Travel Survival Kit* (Lonely Planet).

PEGG LEGG
PUBLICATIONS